MASTERING INSURANCE MARKETING

How to Move Your Agency Forward in the new Media Age

D1173274

Copyright © 2010 by Seth Kravitz and Lev Barinskiy
All Rights Reserved.

InsuranceAgents.com

TABLE OF CONTENTS

Acknowledgements:

This book would not be possible without the contributions of so many wonderful people. We here at InsuranceAgents.com are so thankful to the hundreds of agents who have given us feedback over the years and to the agents who volunteered their time to assist with writhing this book.

In addition, InsuranceAgents.com would never have made it to where we are without the teamwork of our great staff: Lev, Seth, Nate, Suzie, Ann, Chris, Kevin, Andrew, Steve, Al, Mark, James, Bill, Brett, Alex, Shawna, Earl, Ashley, Yogesh, Ashkay, Nicole and so many more who have helped throughout the years.

And finally we would like to thank our editor Matt for being patient with us as we made countless tweaks to this book over the course of seven months.

Introduction:

What You Can Expect From This Book

By Seth Kravitz

My business partner, Lev Barinskiy, and I consider writing this book one of the most important things we have done in our six years here at InsuranceAgents.com. This book sums up hundreds of interactions with agents all across the country and brings the mass of their knowledge into a single, easy-to-read book.

I have met some amazing agents as CEO of InsuranceAgents.com. Some were focused on delivering the best customer service, some focused solely on growth, and some were just simply trying to live a happy life while enjoying what they do. I have visited agencies of all sizes, from agents in their first months of business to one agency with a book of business of $35 million. On average the information in this book is pulled from owners of agencies with books from $1 to 3 million.

You may say, "My agency is much smaller than that," or "I can't relate to those agencies." Regardless of the size, there are many similarities between agencies of all sizes and the knowledge in this book can be applied to an agency of any size. The similar trait they all had, regardless of motive, was that they each had one little secret to their success. Something they prided themselves on that made a true difference. They had something that allowed them to make the jump from an average agency to a great agency.

That's what this book is about. It's about breaking down everything that is no longer working, where the major shifts are in insurance marketing, how to take advantage of them, how to run a super efficient agency, and what the future of this industry will look like in five years. This book will take you on a path to making the changes in your agency processes that will allow you to not only increase your revenue, but also make your clients happier.

I want you to succeed. We didn't choose to name our company InsuranceAgents.com because it was catchy, we chose it because we want to be the leader in insurance marketing and always stay on the cutting edge of what is new in the world of insurance agents. Our success is completely dependent on yours and we want this book to serve as a priceless tool in your new marketing kit.

I get asked all the time by our customers, "What are your successful agents doing to grow?" And my answer has always been rather simple: They never accept that things are as good as they could be. They are always looking for new ways to improve efficiency, raise sales, increase retention, and streamline their agency operations. They aren't afraid to try new things, they give themselves an experimental marketing budget, they ask their customers for feedback constantly, and so on.

Great agencies always want to move onto the next big step. There is a fundamental shift in the way the younger generations are shopping for insurance and in their relationships with their insurance agents. For some of you that may not concern you as your clients may be in their 40's, 50's, 60's or older but the habits of people in their 20's and 30's are steadily climbing through older age groups. The Baby Boomers are becoming more tech savvy with the simplification of technology devices and increasingly their shopping behaviors are starting to resemble those of their children and grandchildren. More people than ever before are shopping for insurance online and researching their agents before they choose one. Being constantly bombarded with messages of comparison shopping and quick online quotes has slowly shifted the mindset of the American consumer.

Every piece of research we could find points to a significant shift toward online shopping and comparison shopping for insurance services. To back up our bold statements we have documented and cited all the research we used throughout the book and you can find references for more information in the footnotes. In our opinion this book is the most heavily researched marketing book written for insurance agents that we know of.

Not only does this book cover what we have learned from insurance agents, but it also covers what we do internally in our own marketing efforts that really work. We share a lot of the secrets to our amazing growth from a three-person operation in 2004 to the 24th-fastest growing company in the US according to Inc Magazine. In addition, we have extensive knowledge of building websites, social media profiles, and email campaigns for our agency customers. All of this collective knowledge can be found not only in this book, but also in our private book-buyers-only section of the site which was included with your purchase.

Lev and I have poured our hearts and souls into this book. We hope it not only meets, but exceeds your expectations and we wish you the best with the success of your agency.

Chapter 1:

Why Traditional Marketing No Longer Works

Experts who give seminars about business love to start their presentations with blanket statements to the effect of, "Forget everything you know about marketing." A lot of times, those statements are simply rhetorical devices, ways to get you to perk up and pay attention to a presentation that hashes over the same old marketing tricks and techniques that you've known for years.

But right now, as the very idea of marketing is changing completely, a phrase like that – one that effectively clears the board on the marketing strategies of the past – isn't only pertinent, it's necessary. You really do need to forget everything you know about traditional marketing, because it's on its way out.

In his book *A History of Marketing Thought*, Robert Bartels categorizes marketing ideas by decade, starting in the 1900s, with the basic concepts, through the 1970s, where it became necessary to adapt

8

marketing to changing societal ideas and social change became a marketing tool itself. All along the way, Bartels argues that marketing has become more specialized and scientific as systems, management structures and environments grow more complex and the demands of an increasingly media-savvy audience shift.[1]

In the last decade or two, that shift has accelerated more rapidly than it ever has before.

Of course, marketing goes back much further than the start of the 20th Century. Town criers promoted events and other goings-on in ancient times. The invention of the printing press in the mid-1400s led to the extensive use of brochures and flyers. Newspapers and magazines revolutionized information distribution and advertising in the 18th and 19th centuries. Spam existed – on the telegraph – in the 1860s, the same decade billboards first became popular. Trademarks started to be widely used for branding products in the 1880s. And the 20th Century brought a marketing revolution with radio, television, systemized phone calls, and the academic study of marketing as a discipline.

---

[1] Bartels, Robert. *A History of Marketing Thought..* 1976.
Summary available at
http://people.missouristate.edu/ChuckHermans/Bartels.ht
m.

All these old methods are becoming obsolete, as the most profound change in marketing and communication since the advent of the printing press takes hold. This is happening even as the basic strategies and goals of marketing – targeting an audience to whom one can promote and distribute a product, setting a price for that product and offering support services that enhance or increase the product's value – remain the same.

Why are the older forms of marketing dying out? One reason, put simply, is that the venues are changing. The old ways of getting your message out to customers – newspapers, magazines, TV, radio, the yellow pages, door-to-door sales, telemarketing – are declining in popularity at a steady pace.

Let's take a look at the numbers.

- Between 1998 and 2007, the percentage of American adults that read newspapers fell from about 58 percent to about 48 percent, according to the Newspaper Association of America.[2] And numbers continue to fall for most papers. In 2009, the Washington Post reported only 13

---

[2] Found at
http://www.naa.org/TrendsandNumbers/Readership.aspx

percent of Americans buy daily newspapers, compared to 31 percent in 1940. [3]

- Magazines are in the same boat. A survey by the Pew Research Center for People and the Press found that 23 percent of people in 2008 said they had read a magazine the day before. In 1994, the number was 33 percent. [4]

- According to the Television Business Report, people watch as much TV as they ever did, but the increasing number of channels has spread viewership of particular shows and particular channels very thin, as audiences have become increasingly fragmented. [5] The highest-rated TV shows have much smaller audiences now. In other words, if you buy advertising time on one station or one show, you won't get as many eyes on your ad as you could a decade or two ago.

- A survey by Paragon Media Strategies found that 73 percent of people ages 14 to 24 nationwide listen to music through sources

---

[3] Ahrens, Frank. "The accelerating decline of newspapers." *The Washington Post*. Oct. 27, 2009.

[4] From http://www.stateofthemedia.org/2009/narrative_magazines_audience.php?cat=2&media=9.

[5] TV Business Report, "Television viewing becomes increasingly fragmented with consumption." http://www.rbr.com/media-news/research/14148.html.

other than broadcast radio. 85 percent of teenagers don't listen to radio. [6]

- Phone directory publishers insist that about 75 percent of adults still use the yellow pages, [7] but that group is getting older and younger customers are more and more likely to go directly to the Internet to find the phone numbers and other information they need. Many environmental groups are trying to get rid of printed phone books altogether, or at least make it so that customers opt-in to getting a printed book.

- The United States Bureau of Labor Statistics projects that the number of door-to-door salespeople and telemarketers will "decline rapidly" over the next decade or so, likely in favor of online marketing strategies. [8]

Other traditional types of advertising and marketing – billboards, door-to-door flyers, etc. – can still be marginally effective, but, as always, the rate of return remains minimal. For every hundred or so people who see your billboard, maybe one or two will

---

[6] Harden, Mark. "Radio's audience dwindling, survey says." *Denver Business Journal*. Nov. 9,2007.
[7] Found at ypassociation.org.
[8] Found at http://www.bls.gov/oco/oco20053.htm.

actually remember your agency the next time that viewer decides to shop for insurance.

The audience is fracturing. Markets are shrinking into smaller and smaller niches. Mass media simply isn't as massive as it used to be. And as that fragmentation continues, marketers are seeing diminishing returns on their ad buys and other mass-media-dependent strategies.

Speaking of the audience, the people who receive your marketing messages have changed immensely over the past few years. Not only in the way that they buy things and seek out products and services, but in the way that they obtain messages, respond those messages and interact with them.

In the period where newspapers, radio and TV were the main venues through which customers took in marketing messages, the communication was largely one-way. Viewers took in marketing messages as basically passive observers, left to their own devices as to whether or not to move forward with buying something or subscribing to a service. The message of an advertisement, commercial or sign was all the customer had to go on, beyond what their friends and family had to say about it.

That's not the case anymore, as your audience and your customers are more involved in the process of determining just what they buy, how they buy it and who they buy it from than ever before. We'll get more into the details of why customers' attitudes are changing in the next chapter – in short, it's about having more say due to increased interactivity spurred by the Internet.

Chapter 2:

The Future of Marketing

Customers want more from the products and services now than they ever have in the past.

It's not enough just to be the neighborhood insurance agent with the office closest to the customer's home. It's not enough to simply have a big company's name on the sign outside your office. It isn't enough to have been in your community for a dozen or two dozen years. Even in this new tougher economy, it's not even enough to outright have the lowest price.

It's about being the total package for the customer, and fitting that customer's specific needs. It's about filling a niche, and clicking with a customer not only in terms of the products you sell and the service you provide but also with your personality and reputation in the community you serve. Customers have seemingly infinite resources now at their fingertips to find out who they're buying from, who else is out there and what agencies might best fit their very specific lifestyles. They can check in with friends on social networking sites and read reviews on business review sites to see just what sort of businesses they'll be dealing with.

In short, customers are no longer just looking for businesses they see in TV ads or in their newspaper or on a billboard every day when they drive to work. They want to give their business to people they think are like them, people who won't only sell them what they want but understand why they're buying it, know how they'll use it and can inform them of the best ways to use the product to further their goals.

But you have an advantage, too, in that the new resources of the web and the new paradigm those resources create allow you to shape how your agency is viewed publicly, infuse it with your own personality and attract those customers that click with your ethos for selling insurance and providing assistance to customers.

Using the Internet and building your reputation in your community are now the keys to effectively moving that message forward. And, unlike marketing strategies of the past, your initial message isn't the end of the exchange. Customers now expect a conversation. They want their questions answered quickly and want to be able to talk – not even necessarily about business, it could be about a TV show or just joking around –

with the person who is sending messages into their Facebook news feeds. The language of marketing isn't one-sided anymore. It's no longer the equivalent of someone with a bullhorn talking to a crowd; now it's more like a party line call where everyone can contribute to what's being said and has equal say in the process.

The advent of desktop publishing in the mid-1980s started the democratization process for marketing and advertising, giving people who previously didn't have the ability to print flyers that ability, plus a venue through which they could preview newspaper advertisements, banners and so forth.[9] But the real revolutions would come in the next decade, as the Internet began to flourish. Suddenly, the ability to send marketing messages was in everyone's hands, from the smallest of businesses to the largest of worldwide conglomerates. Viral marketing – a technique by which videos, clips, images and other content gets passed around among users online – and guerrilla marketing – smaller-scale promotional efforts that focus on imaginative concepts and interactivity – have become widely accepted and used, even by

---

[9] Mirabito, Michael M. *The New Communications Technologies: Applications, Policy and Impact*. 2004. p. 200. Portions available at http://books.google.com.

multinational giants as mass media has declined, and continues to fall off.

In essence, the playing field has been made much more level. Money is no longer the main arbiter of whether a message will get to a receptive audience. Now, creativity, enthusiasm and the ability to get your audience involved can do far more than throwing millions of dollars into radio and TV advertising.

At the same time the Internet revolution has been taking place, several other big changes have been making their way through the world of marketing as well. Integrated marketing and integrated marketing communication – in short, holistic approaches to marketing that start from one key brand identity and aim to promote in all venues in support of that identity – have become accepted as real marketing science, and many universities offer it as a track for marketing students. Integrated marketing plays into Internet marketing in a large way, as many online efforts are focused on brand identification and creating a brand personality. It also aims toward niche, specialized media and uses approaches based on audience data. It shies away from mass-market approaches.[10]

---

[10] Schultz, D. E. "Integrated Marketing Communications: The Status of Integrated Marketing Communications Programs in the US Today," *Journal of Promotion Management*, Vol.1, No.1. 1991, pp.99-104.

Meanwhile, relationship marketing, which focuses on customer retention and satisfaction, and customer relationship management have become guiding forces behind the marketing strategies of the past two decades. As competition within markets grows, the applications for relationship marketing have become more relevant, according to experts. Unlike the marketing strategies of the 1950s and 1960s, which focused more on selling products with lower values to huge numbers of customers, today's marketing approaches look to add value to products being sold. A large part of that effort comes through relationships built between businesspeople and customers.[11]

Customer relationship management looks to streamline and standardize the process of keeping customers satisfied. It includes efforts like 24-hour customer service, technical support and analyzing customer data.

The culmination of all these trends is happening right now, and it's been accelerated by the growing importance of the web in business and commerce. The entire nature of marketing and sales has changed to one based on relationships with specific

[11] Gordon, Ian. *Relationship Marketing: New Strategies, Techniques and Technologies to Win the Customers You Want and Keep Them Forever.* 1999.

customers who build buying experiences that match their own needs and quirks. Rather than migrating toward the most popular or most easily available product on the market, customers now look for brands and ideals that match their own.

But customers aren't the only ones you're going to need to appeal to.

In Adrian Payne's 1991 model, there are six markets which are key to relationship marketing: internal markets, recruitment markets, supplier markets, customer markets, referral markets and influence markets.[12]

- Internal: Appeals to employees to make sure they are working toward the same goals, as well as employees as customers.

- Recruitment: Appeals to potential employees with the correct skills and attributes.

- Supplier: Appeals to those producing and supplying the product.

- Alliance: Appeals to partners who provide idea-based support.

---

[12] Peck, Helen; Chartered Institute of Marketing; Christopher, Martin, Payne, Adrian. *Relationship Marketing: Strategy and Implementation.* p. 416. 1999. Portions available at http://books.google.com.

- Referral: Appeals to customers and non-customers who could refer your agency.

- Influence: Appeals to powerbrokers, including government agencies, unions, financial analysts, stockholder, etc.

- Customer: Appeals to current and potential customers.

Creating a marketing mix that appeals to all six of those markets – not just customers – is important, experts tend to believe. Your marketing approach needs to touch on all those groups, while remaining consistent in terms of your brand.

You may be asking, "How do these ideas, which seem to be focused on big business, apply to me?" And that's a totally valid concern. For a small agency, it's not a priority to appeal to unions or government agencies. But Payne's main point, and one that applies to all businesses, is the need to be aware that an effective marketing strategy is one that will take into account multiple audiences: Your customers, your peers, the people you work with, potential employees, and so on.

Obviously, your main focus is going to be on customers, and that's probably where you're going to want to put the majority of your attention. But an awareness that other important groups are going to be looking at how you're marketing yourself – especially in the areas online where all those different groups converge – is important and worthwhile to have. A blog post you write directed at customers could also include information that would be pertinent to other agents, for instance, or you may link in a post on a social media site to a news story that could mean something worthwhile to both your customers and to local business or community leaders.

Your approach should include a number of different marketing venues and techniques. We'll give you an overview of those venues in the next chapter.

Chapter 3:

Types of Marketing That Will Work in the Future

We've now firmly established that the old, traditional forms of marketing that focus on mass media – TV ads, newspaper ads, radio spots, etc. – are rapidly losing their effectiveness. And that means you're going to have to look toward alternatives to get your name out to the six markets we mentioned in the last chapter, which include customers, suppliers, influencers, referrers, partners and employees. So here we will introduce some techniques that better fit into the new paradigm of focused promotion, niche audiences, and more emphasis on identity and personality, which we'll flesh out more in the following chapters.

Referrals

As mass media declines, people are becoming increasingly more likely to turn to their own personal networks – online, at home, at work or in their communities – than to television, the yellow pages or other mass media outlets for information about businesses and services to turn to. The circles are shrinking. If anything, one of the most important types marketing has is one of the oldest forms that has ever existed, and what people often say is one of the best: word of mouth.[13]

The difference now is that customers, business associates, influencers and others have more ways than ever available to them to find out which agencies have the best reputations, what they can offer and whether those agencies are a good fit for specific niche interests. Not only do they have their friends, their families and their co-workers, they also now have their friends on various social media sites, blog readers, posters on message boards, and the collective opinions of folks who frequent ratings sites such as Yelp, Yahoo! Local and Google Maps to rely on.

But that means you have more options, too. You have more ways to get people you encounter in day-to-day business to tell the people they know about what you do, what you offer and how it can improve people's lives. Use that diversity. If someone isn't willing to talk face-to-face with family about your

---

[13] Information about fracturing mass media audiences found at http://marketing.about.com/od/publicrelation1/a/massm ediapr.htm.

agency, he or she might give you a five-star review online.

It can't hurt to ask.

Social Networking and Blogging

One of the biggest buzz topics in business right now is social networking, the practice of users sharing links, talking to one another and catching up via web-based tools available through personal computers, mobile phones and now tablet PCs like the iPad. People can't stop talking about it and its effect on how business is done. Some are saying it's the new face of marketing and is here to stay; others dismiss it as a fad.

And as much as it may seem to be the realm of teenagers, and despite how quickly social networking has exploded, the honest truth is that it is most certainly not going away. Social networking is becoming more and more ingrained in how people, young and old, live their lives. While sites like Facebook got their start appealing to mainly younger users (Facebook was originally only for college students), older users are signing up for accounts every day (the fastest growing demographic on Facebook is women over 55).[14] And those original college students that used the site are now heading into their 30s, a time

---

[14] Found at
http://www.insidefacebook.com/2009/02/02/fastest-growing-demographic-on-facebook-women-over-55/.

in which they're far more likely to buy homes, start families and need better coverage than they had in their 20s. Their concerns and priorities will change, but their habits when it comes to the web probably won't.

Every day, hundreds of millions of users log on to social networking sites (we'll get into the details of the differences between specific sites later on) and spend their time not only talking about their daily lives with friends and playing various games, but also asking about which products to buy, reviewing services/restaurants/businesses in their neighborhood and seeking advice for big decisions, including buying insurance.

These conversations are going on whether you're involved or not. People will talk about the type or types of insurance you sell, the company or companies whose insurance you sell, and maybe even your agency itself, on the web.

The question is, do you want to participate in those conversations as they happen? If you want to put a good face on your agency and what you do, you more than likely will. We've seen the results that can come from using social networking to promote your agency. They are sizable, and growing at an incredible speed.

And now, as fewer people are turning toward television and newspapers for information, brand identities are being formed online. Wouldn't you want to be a player in how your identity is shaped?

Sales Leads

Leads get you two things that traditional advertising can't guarantee: receptive customers, and their contact information. Thousands of people might look at the same billboard every day, but how many will actually notice it? One percent? Less?[15]

Spending a portion of your promotional budget on leads will deliver you the information for customers who have expressed an interest in changing their insurance or buying it for the first time. You won't have to worry about the group of people that isn't interested. Every lead comes from an expression of interest, which means at least part of the work – finding customers with an interest in what you sell – is done for you.

Of course, that doesn't mean that there's not still plenty of work to do between gaining that information and closing the sale, which we'll get to later.

Getting Involved in Your Community

It's an unusual time for marketing. With the diminished importance of mass media marketing,

---

[15] Found at http://www.socialedge.org/blogs/kiva-chronicles/archive/2008/06/11/the-billboard-bump.

businesspeople must appeal to niches in every way available to them. Some solutions – such as using Internet leads or social networking sites – are high-tech. Others are decidedly old-fashioned.

Making a name for themselves in their communities is something business owners have done since small business has existed, and it's still as effective as it's always been. In conjunction with the brand identity you create online, your real-life presence in your immediate community can shape how people perceive you immensely. If people see you doing good in the place you live, they'll know that you're an honest and altruistic businessperson, too.

There's nothing better for your book of business than a good reputation.

Relationship Building

In all these different forms of marketing, the key thing that you're doing is establishing relationships with customers and others around you. And business relationships, at their heart, aren't really all that different from the relationships you maintain with your friends and family every day. Stay honest and trustworthy, don't turn your back on people that trust you, and stay interested in what others are doing. That's all there is to it.

A long-term approach that focuses on maintaining relationships over turning around a quick buck will always pay off. We've seen it.

And that's a very important thing to keep in mind as you continue through this book. None of what we're talking about is instantaneous. If you picked this book up looking for a way to get rich quick, you got the wrong one. Our interest is in keeping you and your agency profitable and viable into the distant future.

We hope the next few chapters help that interest become a reality.

Chapter 4:

Establishing a Social Media Presence

In less than a decade, social media and social networking have entirely changed the face of marketing and communication. They're the driving force behind a brand new paradigm, one that has more to do with personal connections between clients and service providers and less with top-down advertising messages presented through mass media sources.

For anyone hoping to move forward in business in the future, as social networking becomes an even-more-prevalent part of daily life for millions of people worldwide, an understanding of social media is a necessity. We've already seen what using social media sites can do to make an insurance agency grow. That trend is only going to continue.

For the sake of some perspective, here's an idea of how pervasive social media has become, from digital marketing and e-commerce community Econsultancy (all data is current as of July 2010)[16]:

- Facebook, the largest worldwide social network, has more than 450 million active users worldwide. In mid-2009, the user count was 250 million, so that should give you an idea of the extreme growth of social media usage.

- About half of Facebook's active users log onto the site every day.

- Around 10 percent of Facebook users update their status every day.

- More than 65 million Facebook users access the site through mobile devices such as iPhones and Blackberries.

- More than 700,000 businesses have Facebook pages.

- Twitter has 75 million user accounts, about 15 million of which are regular, active users. That's up from about 10 million global users in 2009.

- The average number of tweets per day is nearly 30 million.

---

[16] Available at http://econsultancy.com/blog/6205-revised-mind-blowing-social-media-statistics-revisited-and-20+-more.

- LinkedIn has more than 50 million members. That number has increased by about 1 million a month since mid-2009.

But you can't expect to harness these exponentially growing tools by simply signing up for an account and expecting customers to flock to you. You have to know completely what social networking is and what it isn't, what your potential customers on social media sites expect, and do your research.

Understanding Social Media

What's the difference between "social media" and "social networking?" Essentially, social media describes the tools users utilize to do social networking. To put it another way, social networking is the act of sharing information and communicating online, while social media sites are the venues for that worldwide conversation.

That's an important word: conversation. That's what social media is: One big conversation. Or, more accurately, it's millions of smaller conversations going on in one big place.

And everything that happens in that huge forum for communication, you've probably done before. If you've ever given someone advice or asked for it yourself, given or received a recommendation, collaborated on a project or worked with a group, or had any shared experience, you've participated in a form of social networking. The only difference between that type of interaction and what people do on Facebook and Twitter is that the latter uses technology to connect people; the former just happens in person.

And just like in-person interaction, online social networking is not one-way communication. It's more like call-and-response. Back-and-forth. For every message you send, you could potentially expect to get as many as dozen or more responses – both good and bad. Or, if you get off to a bad start, and turn people off with an offensive or inappropriate statement, everything you do from then on could land with a resounding thud.

For most casual users, a social media profile is something they consider to be their own personal space, where they can keep up with friends and family, talk about things they like, play games, even get the daily news. Most don't want that space invaded by spammers or advertisers who seemingly do nothing but make noise in their news or Twitter feeds. If you were to jump right into someone's Twitter or Facebook feed with talk about all the great deals and great service you can offer, you'll probably get defriended, unfollowed or blocked. It would be the equivalent of stepping in the middle of someone else's family picnic and trying to sell policies there. You'd get angry looks at best, and most likely kicked to the curb.

Social networking is a permission-based mode of communication. To get anywhere with it, you have to gain people's permission to communicate with them. If you spend some time making yourself a member of a community, really finding ways to fit in and be a genuine member of the group, you would find it a lot easier to get people's attention. They might even tell their friends and families about you and the service you offer. In fact, that's happening right now. Lots of major brands, including Southwest Airlines, Starbucks, Zappos, Comcast, IBM and Dell, have leveraged Twitter, Facebook and company blogs into highly followed presences that people interact with and trust. [17]

You can, too.

Why Do It?

It's common for people resistant to social networking to come up with lots of objections to getting involved in the practice. Maybe they think it's a fad that's going to go away, or they think they don't have the time. Perhaps they think it's not relevant to their businesses or they'd prefer their staff to spend

---

[17] Solis, Bryan. "The Essential Guide to Social Media." 2008. http://www.briansolis.com/2008/06/essential-guide-to-social-media-free/.

time on other things. Possibly they're worried about errors and omissions, as well as a lacking return on their investments.

But those are excuses and dodges. Fears of not accepting the new paradigm.

Social media is here to stay. And the benefits outweigh the arguments against investing one's time. Social media serves as:

- A place to build relationships with the customers you'll be serving.
- A way to contact customers immediately and directly.
- An ever-growing tool for communication that more and more people are using as a primary way to keep in touch.
- A way to engage customers on a personal level.
- An organic way to generate leads and referrals.
- A venue for addressing customer concerns and answering questions quickly.

Getting Started

The basics of social networking are fairly easy. It's simply talking and interacting with people, just as you do every day, through a website or a phone application.

Just like many things it can be easy to learn but difficult to master. It's important for you to learn the language not only of the specific sites where you'll be communicating with customers and others, but also of the individual communities you hope to join.

Doing the Research

You should take some time to study what's going on at the sites you do decide are the social media venues you plan to use. As we said earlier in the chapter, learn the language. Social media sites all have their own unique lingo that users employ as a sort of shorthand between each other.

For instance, on Twitter, there are hashtags (phrases preceded with a # to make them easily searchable), RTs (retweets, or repeating something another user said), trending topics (popular discussion items) and lots of other bits of jargon you need to know to be conversant.

But there's another reason why it would be beneficial to do some reconnaissance on social media sites before really getting involved in the discussions there. You need to learn the culture. The etiquette. What flies on LinkedIn, a site specifically designed for businesspeople to connect with one another, may not on Facebook, which is geared toward a general audience and is not necessarily intended to be a business environment. In fact, Facebook was originally devised as a way for college students to keep up with other students on their own campuses.

Go to the sites you want to use and see what's going on there; what people are saying and what they enjoy about being there. Then try to fit into that culture.

Defining Your Strategy and Goals

What image do you want to portray via social networking sites?

It's important to know, and to make sure that everyone who is going to be helping you with your social networking venture knows before you start using the sites, so that you present a strong brand image and a unified message. What kind of message you present will depend mainly on what outcomes you'd like to see from using social media. Are you:

- Just testing the waters to see what using social media can do?
- Trying to find ways to counter unfavorable word-of-mouth or publicity?
- Looking to acquire leads so you can make sales?
- Hoping to provide better service to existing customers?
- Planning to expand your market share?

All of these are attainable goals through social networking, but each one is conducive to a different audience and different types of social networking sites.

According to Lena West, CEO and chief strategist at xynoMedia, it's important to fit social media into your schedule and marketing strategy. Just trying to cram it in there with everything else you're doing won't work – cut out what's not working and fit your social networking into those spots. West also suggests scheduling time to do your social networking activity. If it's a priority, you'll put it on your calendar.

Another worthwhile tip from West: Be wary of "experts." If someone claims to be an expert in social media but it isn't his or her profession, he or she isn't worth listening to. And even if the expert writes and consults about social media, you can't listen to them all. Pick those you think give the best advice and stick with them, as listening to too many sources will just lead to conflicting ideas.

Picking Your Venues

There are literally hundreds, if not thousands, of social media websites on the Internet. To try to get involved in all of them, or even a large number of them, would be futile. To even try to get involved with every site that you think may hold potential customers in your area or that you think relates to the insurance industry would be biting off more than you can chew.

It's best to pick two or at most three sites – some bigger ones such as Facebook, Twitter or LinkedIn and one or two with an industry focus – and place your attention there. Maybe start with one and once you have that presence satisfactorily set up, move on to another.

But beyond all else, it's important for you to remember not to overextend yourself. If you find yourself lacking the time to regularly check or update your social media profiles, it's probably not worth the effort to have them. Don't create profiles that you can't keep up with on a regular basis.

Remember your goals. If your main goal is to test the water and see what social networking can accomplish, you may want to start with a smaller, niche site. If you want to improve your business contacts or your agency mainly caters to business clients, a site like LinkedIn is probably the best. If you want to get your message to a broad audience of potential clients and want to speak to them in a personal way, Facebook or Twitter might be preferable.

Know your audience. And study the demographics of the various social networking sites you might want to use. Wherever you see the biggest overlap in users and your potential customer base, aim in that direction. Also, you can get a good idea of where your customers are online by simply asking them what sites they use.

About the Biggest Sites

Facebook

Facebook is a social media site that allows users to connect with "friends," with whom they may then share comments, photos, videos and links. Users create specific pages for themselves where they list interests and other information about themselves. Businesses can create "fan pages" for their brands. Users can become fans of those pages and interact with the company there. It's the largest social networking site in the world, so odds are many of your clients already use it.

Tips:

- Post pictures so people can seen the personal, human side of your agency.
- "Tag" pictures with people's names. If you tag a client in a photo, their friends will see that and your agency will be more visible.
- Monitor your Facebook page for unwanted content or complaints. Respond politely. Others

may come to your aid, but you need to be there to participate.

- Keep a dialog going. Talk about safe topics other than your business. Maybe sports, local activities or interesting news articles.

Twitter

Twitter allows users to post short messages of 140 characters in real-time. Other users ("followers") can then respond to those messages in directed "tweets." Various third party websites also allow users to post pictures, videos and longer messages.

Tips:

- Twitter allows you to post information in real-time, so it's a good place to make announcements.

- You can also answer customer questions and have a dialog about their concerns.

- Twitter's "list" function allows you to organize your followers and the people you follow into groups, such as customers or other professionals.

- Like Facebook, Twitter gives you the opportunity to share links to interesting content.

LinkedIn

Similar to Facebook in functionality, LinkedIn is a social media site specifically geared toward business professionals and which can serve as a sort of online resume. Users can recommend other users as a sort of professional seal of approval.

Tips:

- Get involved in groups. It's a good way to network with other professionals.

- Recommend people you know. Maybe you'll get recommendations back.

YouTube

Not exactly a social networking site per se, YouTube does offer a venue for you to upload videos, which you can then place on Facebook, link to on Twitter or post on your company blog.

Concerns About Errors and Omissions

Perhaps the biggest question businesspeople go into social networking with has to do with what risks are inherent in participating. Are you leaving yourself open to lawsuits by using such sites? Is it possible you could be violating any ethics codes or breaking any laws by what you say?

Follow these guidelines and you should be protected from harm while using social media to boost your agency.

Know and Obey Specific Site Rules

Most social networking sites have privacy policies and/or user agreements that very clearly lay out all the things that they allow and do not allow. Among the things most do not allow are spamming users, sending harassing messages, claiming to be someone you aren't and having multiple accounts. Carefully read these policies to ensure that you are using the site to specifications.

Be Aware of the Possibility of Defamation

Much like print or broadcast media, social media and blogs can be fertile territory for defamation, especially when it comes to commercial or advertising speech. Consult with an attorney to make sure what you're saying is fair and will not be.

You Can't Blame the Site

Most social media site user agreements include clauses that indemnify them from any responsibility in the event of harm to a user.

Know Your State Law Regarding Advertising

In many states, Internet advertising is governed under the same law as standard advertising through billboards, radio and TV. There are still some unanswered questions as to what exactly constitutes online advertising – such as whether a profile page itself is an ad or if it's just an advertising message – but it would be best for you to assume that everything you do could be considered an ad.

Use Disclaimers

When you give advice or perform professional services via social networking sites, it's important for you to use the standard disclaimers you do for phone and e-mail communication or on your website. Let all your employees know that any discussion on a social networking site must go through a standard process and workflow to avoid potential risks.[18]

How Agencies Are Already Using It

Just like the brands we mentioned earlier, many insurance agencies are now using social networking sites to solidify their own brands and get their messages out to huge number of potential customers.

Take, for example, Rey Insurance Agency in upstate New York. Agent Linda Rey has acquired thousands of Twitter followers, has posted multiple YouTube videos and collected hundreds of Facebook

---

[18] Found at
http://www.iiaba.net/na/16_AgentsCouncilForTechnology
/NA20090715142908?ContentPreference=NA&ActiveState=
AZ&ContentLevel1=ACT&ContentLevel2=&ContentLevel3
=&ActiveTab=NA&StartRow=0.

fans. On those sites, Ms. Rey doesn't just talk about insurance, though she does do plenty of that, she also displays her personality and makes a personal connection with customers, making jokes about her workday, linking to relevant articles, talking about local issues like traffic.

She put a human face on her agency. That can make a huge amount of difference.

Other agencies, such as Vaughn Insurance Agency Company in Kentucky, are using blogs to get their message out and interact with clients and potential customers.

About Blogs

Blogs have been around a little longer than the big social networking sites and as a result have a little more of a traditional feel than those sites do. Essentially, your agency's blog will be the place where you can post long-form writing about what you're doing, who your customers are, and what your philosophy is. You don't have to be a great writer to maintain a successful blog; you only have to get your points across clearly and be open with your readers.

Some tips for making the most of your blog:

- Set up a calendar for your posts, so that you can remind yourself to post about the incoming tornado season, impending winter weather or other annual events.

- Have multiple authors. The more content you can generate, the better.

- But stay consistent. Nobody wants to read a blog post that doesn't tell him or her anything worthwhile or that is impossible to understand.

- Keep your posts relatively short.

- Don't go too far in one direction between personal and professional.

What Social Networking Is and Isn't

With the right approach, using social media sites can get you more customers, build your professional relationships and improve your reputation in the marketplace. What it won't do is transform your agency overnight. Just like any real-life friendship or professional relationships, your connections through social media will take some time to build up. But they'll pay off immensely.

That's your initial return on your investment: Relationships. Eventually, those will turn into profit, if you log on to each social networking site you use with a goal each time, whether it be to gain another follower, send something of interest to the followers you have, or just answer a question in a helpful way.

Chapter 5:

Referrals

It's one of the oldest clichés in marketing and business to say that word of mouth is the most effective form of advertising. But unlike many of the old rules of marketing, this one still holds true.

People are more likely to take advice from friends, family and co-workers than they are some billboard they see or a TV advertisement or a radio ad. Trust is timeless.

In fact, business gained through customers referring you to the people they know may be more important now that it's ever been. Why? Because with the growing power of social networking and the Web, there are so many more venues for people to discuss and recommend businesses they like. Certain websites, such as Yelp.com, Google Maps and Yahoo! Local give users the ability to rate and review businesses they like or don't like. More and more, people moving into a new area check those sites to see whom they should trust and whom they shouldn't, based on other customers' experiences.

So it's very important that you try to get high ratings on those sites, as well as give your customers reason to tell the people close to them that your agency is the place to go for the best possible service.

Why They're Useful

There's a lot to be gained from asking your customers to refer you to people they know. Here are just a few things you can get out of them:

- A cycle of satisfied customers. As an increasing number of clients willing to talk to friends about your agency find themselves happy with your products and services, they'll tell more people about it. Those people, if satisfied, will tell their friends, and they'll tell their friends, and so on.

- Reduced expenses and optimized time. Think about it: When you're getting referrals, other people are doing the work for you. They're doing the work you would be doing if you were spending all day cold-calling prospects or sending out e-mails, but with a much greater chance of success.

- You'll get a better return. Experts say you can expect about a 10 percent return from non-qualified leads, while referred leads can bring you around a 60 percent closure rate. That's six times better!

- They're important for long-term growth. When you start your agency, it's important to gain business from your local market of shoppers, but to keep your business growing years into the future, you'll need those shoppers to be your advocates so you can continue to expand your influence and your customer base.

Customer Referrals

The classic form of referral is one you get from a customer who is also a fan of what you do. Sometimes, customers will volunteer to do this for you on your own, but more likely than not they'll need a nudge from you. Of course, it can cause a little anxiety to ask customers to go out into the world and be your advocates, but you've got to ask the question.

Breaking the Barrier

It can be tough to ask for a referral, especially if you're a person who worries a lot that saying the wrong thing at the wrong time can kill a sale. But if you don't ask, you'll be wasting an opportunity. The key is knowing when to ask and who to ask.

Pick Your Best

Not everyone is going to be a prime candidate for referrals. Someone who is shy, not very well-spoken, who often complains about various things in his/her policy or who is seemingly skeptical about the insurance industry itself probably isn't the best choice for a referrer.

So who is a good choice? Someone who clearly appreciates the product you sell and the service you give. Someone who understands the product and can speak well about it. Someone who has experienced what the benefits of the product are. And, frankly, it helps if he or she is someone with a lot of friends, family members or co-workers to talk to. Think about your top 20 percent. The people you serve who are most in-tune with your business and who really get it. Those are the ones you're really going to want to recruit. But even then, you may need to give them some incentive to help you out.[19]

Make It Easier

Print up a pre-written referral letter that a client could hand to a friend, a family member or a co-worker. Or provide the client with an e-mail template. Or at least give some recommendations for what to

---

[19] Found at http://sbinformation.about.com/cs/advertising/a/aa02020 3a.htm.

say. That gives your client the opportunity to refer your agency without having to figure out ways to word a recommendation. You also want to avoid surprising the client's friend when you call and drop their – maybe former – friend's name. Give the client plenty of time to talk to his or her friend, and confirm that it's OK to call before you pick up the phone. Provide the stamp if the client wants to mail a letter, and always make yourself available to talk on the phone.[20]

Likewise, it's a good idea to offer a product or service that could come up in a day-to-day conversation, which gives your client an in to bring you up. Luckily, insurance – be it health, car, or home – tends to deal with everyday issues.

Offer a Reward

A discount, free promotional items, a special gift certificate or some sort of VIP status are a few of the things you could offer to push your best customers into being more vocal about your agency to their friends or to give you the contact information of some people they know.[21]

---

[20] Found at http://www.insurance-leads-advisor.com/getting-referrals.html.
[21] Found at http://sethgodin.typepad.com/seths_blog/2006/11/how_to_get_refe.html.

In addition, offering rewards for the people being referred to your agency could help your clients make the leap into voicing their recommendations. It gives them something tangible and valuable to offer their friends, beyond simply their word.

But you should be aware that offering to pay a client for a referral can be a risky proposition. At that point, it becomes less an agent/client relationship and more of one of monetary responsibility. You're asking the client to put his or her credibility on the line. That can scare people away.

If you don't want to spend the money it takes to provide rewards or gifts, simply thanking the people who take the time and make the effort to refer your agency can go a long way. Send a personalized e-mail or postcard to let that client know how much you appreciate his or her help.

Reduce the Risk

A client is more likely to refer you if he or she doesn't believe there's too much risk involved, either for the client or the person he or she refers. Don't make it too hard for those people brought in by referrals – maybe include a free trial period or a reduced first-month rate. That way, the person who's referring you won't have to worry about his or her friend accusing him or her of playing a trick or being a shill. The person he or she refers will get a chance to check out your product and services without any obligation, which is often a big barrier to trying out insurance.

If you're not willing to provide such incentives, you'll have to learn to simply understand that you'll really have to earn your referrals. Your customers will have to trust you enough to ask their friends to make the obligation. That's a high hurdle, but one you can cross with enough trust building.

Prove Your Value

Make yourself an agent that people would willingly want to refer. Be attentive to all your clients' needs. Know your status and reputation in your area and within the industry. If it's a good one, maintain it. Build trust with all your clients and always thank them for their business and for referrals.

We'll get more into how you can make progress by treating your customers like people instead of numbers in a later chapter.

Tips For Success

Set a Goal

What do you want out of referrals? To grow your business by 10 percent in six months? To increase your prospects over the next year? A revenue boost? Whatever it is, clearly state what you'd like to accomplish and set a timeline for yourself. Then work toward that. Be motivated.

Target Your Audience

You should know exactly what kind of client you're looking for, in terms of demographics and needs. For instance, if you're selling car insurance, you're obviously only going to want customers who own cars, but you may also only be looking for customers who have certain types of cars, with a particular sort of driving record, or who have been driving for a particular amount of time.

Letting your existing clients know who you're interested in bringing in to your agency will give them an idea of which of their friends and family to recommend to you or to recommend you to.

Gauge the Client

Ask the client how he or she thinks you're doing when it comes to his or her needs. If the client answers enthusiastically, that person is likely a good candidate for referrals. Get an idea of the person's communication style – would he or she be more comfortable giving out a brochure, just conversing? – and ask what he or she might think about asking others if they're interested getting the same great product and service.[22]

If the client answers negatively or declines to answer, hold off. Come back to the topic later, after he

---

[22] Found at http://www.insureme.com/insurance-agent/asking-for-referrals.

or she has had some time to become more familiar with your agency and what you have to offer.

It's a good idea to always take advantage of personal meetings with clients – updates to their policies, renewals, answering general questions – to ask if they know anyone who could benefit from a policy from your agency. People tend to be more receptive in person than over the phone or in e-mails.

Make Referrals Part of the Process

Let clients know upfront that you might be asking them for referrals later on. Tell them that, as a matter of doing business, you would hope they would refer two or three other people to your agency, with the possibility of rewards. That way, you won't end up surprising the client later on when you ask for him or her to bring three referrals in. You might be surprised how many will agree.

Don't be pushy. Some people just want to buy a policy and aren't interested in being an advocate for your agency, at least not yet. Don't scare them away or make them uncomfortable if they balk. Just say that you can talk about referrals more later in the process, when they're more comfortable with what you have to offer.

Use Stickers, Signs and Notices on Printed Material

A sign on your door that states that people like you on Yelp! or a sticker that tells customers to like you on Facebook can be a good prompt to get your name out onto areas of the Web that people who are interested in the products you sell visit. Likewise, buttons on your blog or company website leading customers to those sites could garner you some good reviews, which would lead to a better position when people search for insurance in your area.

Referrals From Colleagues

Depending on what kind of agency you run – whether it's for the general public or more aimed toward business customers – referrals from known professionals could be far more important than those from everyday people. But even if you run an agency that isn't focused on businesses, it could still be very helpful for you to gain a good word from others within your industry and even outside of it. Here's why:

- Customers listen to businesspeople they trust. Say, for instance, someone has a mechanic he or she really trusts and who the customer takes his or her car to on a regular basis. That customer might then ask where a good place is to have a new car stereo installed or get the transmission worked on. Same goes for other industries. If someone has a life insurance agent he or she really likes, that person might turn to that agent to ask for help finding car insurance or health care coverage.

- You'll gain respect among your peers. Being well thought of within your own business community can only bring benefits to your agency. Your competitors will obviously still want to get to customers before you do, but at least there will be a mutual respect between you. Plus, gaining respect among other agents can help you get an influential spot on a local board or within a trade group.

- Word gets around. If you become known as an "agent's agent" other people will look to you as someone who does things the right way.

How To Get Them

You're probably saying to yourself right now, "How am I supposed to get referrals from other insurance agents, many of whom I'm competing against locally?" For one thing, the agents who recommend you might not all be local. If you're a captive agent, you might get a referral from another agent within your company but in another state when one of his or her customers move to your area. Or you could get referrals from agents who focus on different types of insurance.

Some tips:

- Get to know other agents in your company. For a captive agent, it can be very beneficial to know agents in other cities or other states whom you can refer and who can refer you to customers who move.

- Refer others. Independent agents don't have the luxury of being able to get recommendations from inside their companies, so they have to use other methods. One good way to create a community of like-minded agents is to start referring your own customers to agents you like, or even other businesses related to the insurance you sell. For instance, you might tell a customer who the best local dentist is. Or refer him or her to a well-run used car lot. Once those businesspeople know that you referred them to your customers (and a friendly call might be a good way to inform them), they'll be more likely to put in a good word for you.

- Join local business groups. Maybe get involved in your area chamber of commerce or an insurance trade organization. The more you get to know other businesspeople as human beings, the easier it will be for them to recommend you and for you to recommend them.

- Use social networking. It's a good way to get to know business colleagues as well as new potential customers.

Online Referrals

Keep an eye on what people are saying about you online – on Twitter, Facebook, Yelp, Yahoo! Local and other sites. One thing you can do to be aware of what people are saying about your agency is to set up a Google Alert, which sends a daily e-mail to your inbox listing all the mentions of you online in a given day, based on a Google search. Keeping up with online comments gives you a good idea of what customers think about you and your agency, as well as what you could be doing better.

As we mentioned before, you should direct your customers, especially those who you interact with via social networking sites, to leave feedback on those sites and others. That way, when someone searches for the type of insurance you sell on Google, not only will you be one of the top results, you'll also be one of the highest-rated. People put a lot of stock in those ratings.[23]

[23] Found at http://community2.business.gov/t5/Small-Business-Matters/Get-to-the-Top-Tips-for-Making-your-Business-Web-Site-More/ba-p/30963.

One mistake businesspeople sometimes make is to visit a review site and respond to a bad review or a complaint with a defensive tone or, worse yet, a combative one. That's counter-productive. If you choose to respond to your online critics, always do so in a calm, helpful way that aims to make you look like a consummate professional with the tools and skills to solve even the biggest problems. Solving a customer's issue in a public forum is a great way to show people you know what you're doing.

Turning Referrals Into Referrals

The biggest selling point of referrals is the fact that they should, if done right, become a self-perpetuating engine of growth for your agency. Those who get referred by your customers should refer their friends, and they'll refer their friends, and so on. The only things you have to do are provide consistent, high-quality service and products to your customers, and ask for referrals when the time is right. Similarly, referrals from local businesspeople you know can keep bringing customers to your door in perpetuity.

It's all about the long-term.

Chapter 6:

Leads

Leads have been a part of sales for decades now, but there are still a lot of misconceptions about what exactly they are. People tend to think of leads as a card or an e-mail with contact information. An e-mail address to send a form letter to, or a phone number to call with a scripted message. Salespeople often treat leads as data, something to be used to boost a bottom line and plug into a database.

And while leads can do a lot for your bottom line, to view them as something you can simply plug into a system and expect a sale to spit out is an unrealistic and unproductive perspective.

Leads are people.

And people are complicated. Everyone – each name, phone number and e-mail address you get – has his or her own needs, own specific situation and particular questions about what the insurance you're selling can do for his or her life. They're not going to be automatic moneymakers. They take work and cultivation, because people have to be convinced that choosing you is the right decision for them. To you, they may just be another prospect for another sale, but for them, deciding on which insurance to buy and which coverage to get is a very important and daunting choice. They have to be convinced and that takes some work.

Think of each lead like a seed, and of yourself as a gardener. To get a big yield, you have to:

- Plant a lot of seeds, not all of which will turn into healthy plants.

- Do your planting months ahead of your planned harvest.

- Care for the seeds you've planted on a regular basis.

- Adjust for the problems of individual plants – maybe weeds are the problem, or not enough water. Each one is different.

- Keep cultivating what you plant even as it continues to grow. Follow it along through the whole process.

- Don't give up halfway through! That's the easiest way to lose the whole crop.

- Continue buying seeds and planting them from year to year to ensure long-term success.

Leads are just like seeds. Work hard to cultivate them, and you should get a big return.

How to Get Them

There are lots of ways to acquire leads – including, as we mentioned in an earlier chapter, using social networking sites to make contact with new customers. But to get a guaranteed number of leads every month, the best thing to do is buy them from a company that offers competitively priced, fresh leads from willing customers.[24]

Once you decide that you want to buy leads for your agency, you're going to have to make a few decisions about the quantity you buy and the type of customer you're looking for. Here are some practices that will get you the best results, based on our years of experience cultivating, acquiring and selling leads:

Buy enough. A mistake many insurance agents make when they decide to buy leads is to only buy a few to try them out. Frankly, that won't work. You have to buy enough leads to be able to contact a good number of potential customers so that you can keep

---

[24] Found at
http://www.seniormarketadvisor.com/Issues/2010/1/Pag es/50-Best-Ways-to-Generate-Leads.aspx.

bringing new business into your agency. The number will vary depending on the size of the agency you run, but some our most successful clients buy 10 a day – and our experts recommend 10 leads a day per producer for larger agencies.

Don't restrict yourself. When you buy leads, you have the option of setting filters so that the leads you receive come from a specific geographic area and your customers meet certain demographic criteria. It's tempting to set very strict filters for yourself – maybe just your city or only people who earn a certain amount of money each year – but that's not the best move. You want to set very limited filters, for two main reasons: 1) To ensure that you get enough leads to make your effort worthwhile. 2) So you can get a good idea of where your efforts are best focused.

You could, for instance, start out by buying leads from everyone in your state over age 25. After some time, you can check to see what areas and groups of people are bringing your the best return on your investment. You might be surprised what you find out. You could find that your best customers come from an area you weren't even planning to look at.

Remember your competitors. One thing you should be aware of when you buy leads is that other agents in your area may be doing the same thing. And if they are, there's a chance they're getting the same leads as you are. Unless you buy an exclusive lead, which comes with a premium price tag, each lead you buy will be sold to two to three other agents.

What does that mean for you? It means you have to beat your competitors to the punch. It means you need to call leads immediately once you get them. Our research shows it's **20 times** more likely for you to convert a lead to a sale if you call within the first five minutes.[25]

We'll get more into just what you should do when you call a client or when a client calls you in the next chapter.

Keep the others agents in your company in mind. If you're a captive agent, it's important that you note which company you're associated with when you sign up to buy leads. You should also make sure that other agents in your company assign their carrier settings, too. Lead sales firms like InsuranceAgents.com don't sell leads to two agents who work for the same carrier. So don't create any unnecessary competition for yourself.

Not All Leads Are Created Equal

It's important that you go into using leads with realistic expectations. Some leads will turn out to be better than others, and depending on how you speak to

---

[25] Found at
http://www.leadresponsemanagement.org/kellogg_study.

your customers, you will have varying degrees of success. Some things you should be aware of:

Ask for pertinent information. Sometimes a potential client might enter the wrong phone number or some incorrect data that affects the quote. If a client has entered fake information, you can get a refund for those leads. But a typo or a slight mistake may lead to confusion if you don't ask the client some informational questions upfront.

Don't give a quote in a voicemail or email before talking to them. If you offer a quote right away, you do two things that could create problems for you down the road. First, you give the customer a quote that may or may not be accurate, given the incorrect information issues we describe above. Second, you make the conversation strictly about price. Once price is introduced into the conversation, that will be the only factor that matters to the customer. You know full well that there's far more to the policy you're selling than price alone. You should let your customer know that, too. Show him or her the value, then divulge the price.

Don't call the alternate number first. Customers put their primary phone number down for a reason. Perhaps they don't like to be bothered at work or only use their cell phones for emergency calls. Or maybe they prefer not to use their home phones.

Whatever the case, honor the customers' wishes by calling the primary number they put down first. Only after a few tries there should you call the secondary number. Sure, they put down that secondary number, but that doesn't mean they necessarily want you to call it right away.

How to Manage Them

It can be a little disconcerting at first to work with leads. If you're buying a substantive quantity of them, it's easy to feel overwhelmed by all the phone numbers and e-mail addresses coming at you with considerable speed.

And if you try to manage those leads yourself, you might find yourself extraordinarily overworked as you try to enter all your data into an electronic spreadsheet or onto a ledger. Or you might find yourself hiring on more people to do the lead management while you do what you do best – working with customers and writing policies.

So what do you do as an alternative to overworking yourself or paying more salaries? You can buy or subscribe to a lead management system, a software program or a Web-based tool that takes in your leads, organizes them in a readable way, and even updates you when you need to contact a potential customer or follow up with one to whom you've already sold a policy.[26]

Providers including AgencyIQ, ALISS, EZLynx, Vertafore, Typhoon, Mojo, InsideSales.com, Prospector+, Leads360 or Imprezzio have a number of different types of systems that can organize your lead information quickly and easily, and give you more time to simply run your business.

So what type of lead management system should you get? There are lots of options out there. And some systems are better suited to your agency than others. Here are some things to look for as you look for a system and make your final decision about which one to invest in:

- If system generates its own e-mails to send to potential clients.
- Whether all relevant information is easily accessible and can be sorted.
- Whether the system tracks the sources and types of leads you're getting.
- If the system keeps up with conversion rates for the various types of leads.

---

[26] Found at
http://www.leadresponsemanagement.org/mit_study.

- If the system includes a workflow based on insurance industry practices.

- Whether the company that provides the system offers training for best practices.

- What sort of support the company provides.

- If the system is Web-based or requires its own hardware.

- How reliable the system is.

- If the system provides full visibility of your lead history.

- Whether the formatting of the reports the system provides fits your needs.

- If the system integrates with the information sent by lead providers.

The system that might work best for your competitors or for other agents might not be the best fit for your particular agency, so really look into the details of what each system can do and how it best fits in with your workflow. The right one for you is out there, and it can save you an incredible amount of time and money once you implement it.

Here are some other things a lead management system can do for you:

Automate contacts/follow ups. As soon as a lead gets fed into your lead management system, many systems have the ability to immediately send an e-mail to a client thanking them for their interest. That gets your foot in the door and makes the client aware of who you are and that you plan to give him or her a call.

Of course, you'll have to make your own call – and soon – but the software can make that first step.

After you make contact with clients, your lead management system can keep up with what you've done. After a set amount of time, it can remind you to follow up with those clients you spoke to recently so that nobody gets lost in the process.

Any client you fail to follow up with is almost certainly a lost sale. In fact, studies show that companies who regularly and thoroughly follow up with potential clients have closing rates three times higher than those who do not. Many systems can even send their own follow-up e-mails that provide clients with new and useful information. A dialer system can help you manage your follow-up calls as well.

Get the lead to you instantly. Your lead management system will route each lead you buy directly to you and put the information right in front of your face so that you can act on it. The faster you see the lead, the faster you can make contact with the customer and make the sale.

Measure your progress. Many lead management systems have features that allow you to track each lead's place in the sales process. So when you follow up, you can know exactly where it is you left off and avoid the time-consuming process of catching back up.

Also, your content management system can give you a good idea of where you're having the most success. That data could lead you toward improved profitability by helping you to know how to narrow your filters.

Organize information. Leads can come from all sorts of sources – the Web, e-mail, direct mail, referrals, people you connect with via social networking, and so on. A lead management system is a single, centralized place where all your lead information lives. You can live with the assurance that, when you return to it, it'll be organized, updated and easy to cull for the data you need.

You can also use your system to keep up with notes on specific clients so you will always have a place to find the little details that can mean so much in the process of making a sale. You won't have deal with messy or illegible notes scribbled on a note pad next time you call or get caught off-guard with a call from a client.

Drip marketing. Clients may not always respond to the first message you leave them or your initial phone call. But that doesn't mean you should give up on them or that they're not interested.

Your lead management system can help keep them updated by sending periodic, regular messages letting them know all the aspects and benefits of your agency, why it's the best for them and what you can offer. You can provide the customer with new information each time – some aspect of the policy you didn't discuss or an update – and bring him or her closer to a sale.

Keep up with x-dates. For those clients who have already bought policies with your agency, a lead management system can help you know when to make contact that make sure your customers know it's time to renew their policies.

Cost savings. Your lead management system will do the work that you would either end up spending too much of your time doing yourself or that you would have to hire other employees to do. Letting a software program do the organizing and keeping up with important dates frees you up to do what's most important for your agency.

ROI. We know for a fact that leads will eventually pay off. But to get that payoff in an efficient and effective way, you're going to need to be able to manage them in the best way possible, especially if you're calling 20 to 30 leads per day, the number experts recommend for agents.

Keep up with competitors. Many of your competitors who use leads already have lead management systems in place. To keep up with other agencies in your area and to make sure that you are the agent who contacts the client first, you'll need one of your own, preferably a better one than the ones your competitors are using.

Keys to Success

Some agents make mistakes when they buy leads. They don't know how to use them to the best effect. They let them sit for days before they call or they focus on too small an area or group. As a result, those agents get impatient and give up on leads, feeling disillusioned and frustrated.

Don't be that agent. As we mentioned earlier in the chapter, two of the major ways to make leads work for you are to contact potential clients quickly and make sure you buy enough leads to make your investment valuable. But there are some other things you should do – or more importantly, not do – to make leads work better for you.

Don't give up on them. It may seem obvious to simply say, "see it through," but a lot of agents expect sales leads to be the equivalent of a get-rich-quick scheme. They anticipate that their agencies will grow immensely in just a few weeks. That's just not realistic. It takes time and patience to really make leads pay off.

Don't Be Pushy. Agents who get impatient may feel a need to prod their customers to make a decision more quickly. That's a mistake. The harder you push your customers, the more you'll push them away. Give them room to breathe and time to decide, stay patient, and your work will be worth it.

Don't assume. Jumping to conclusions is a common reaction to a lack of response from a client or less-than-expected return, but you have to fight the urge to decide that customer simply bought from somebody else or that leads just won't work for you. Keep asking, keep making contact and keep buying leads until you have a definitive answer. If a customer raises objections, don't assume that they're probably going to walk out your door. People can have genuine questions, even if they do plan on buying. Hang in there, provide good answers and avoid being defensive. If you can impress the client with what you know and don't get confrontational, the conversation should continue.

Don't settle. It may be tempting to keep the number of leads you buy at the same level well beyond the point that your agency has grown and expanded, or to even reduce them after you reach an initial growth goal. That's short sighted. To continue growing, you should keep the number of leads you buy over time at a steady pace.

Work the weekend. Try upping your lead flow on Saturday and Sunday. Since lots of agents take those days off, you'll have less competition, even though lots of people will choose those days to go online and search for insurance quotes. People also tend to be more available to talk on the weekend, so you likely won't be butting into a customer's busy schedule.

Turn leads into more leads through cross selling. Say, for instance, that one of your customers is shopping for life insurance. Have him or her fill out a form with some questions about just what the customer is looking for in a policy. Then ask if he or she might have an interest in other types of insurance you sell. You could use that information to cross-sell another policy. Then, ask that lead if he or she might be interested in referring you to others. Keep the cycle going.

Chapter 7:

Making Contact

No matter how you get a customer's contact information – be it a lead, a referral or the customer simply walks into your office – virtually nothing is more important for your agency than communicating with your clients. And not just at the beginning, though making that first contact can make or break your sale. It's imperative that you stay in touch with your customers through the entirety of the sales process and even after you make the sale. The thing that will set you apart from other agents is your ability to communicate and care.

You'll want to use every tool for communication available to you – e-mails, phone calls, voicemails, in-person conversations, social media channels – to continue to build your relationships with your customers.

Using the Phone

The communication tool you likely use the most in the course of running your agency is the telephone. So you need to get comfortable with it, and get good at letting customers know who you are and what you have to offer without them being able to see you, with just a few words. If you're not comfortable, the customer won't be, and it's imperative that you earn the customer's trust.

Here are some ways you can use the phone more effectively when you're the one making the initial call:

Call as soon as you can. As we mentioned earlier, the sooner you call after getting a customer's contact information, the more likely you'll beat your competitors and make the sale.

Start strong. You have just a few seconds to hook the customer and get him or her as involved in the conversation as you are. So show your personality right away. That way, the customer knows that you're a dynamic person and not a boring number cruncher or an automated calling service. The customer can't see you or your body language, so they will judge you by your tone of voice and the words you use. You need to be likable so that the customer will feel comfortable giving you their business.

Prove you're an expert. Customers expect you to know what you're selling and know what's best for their personal situations. They want someone who will give them guidance toward the right policy. Prove you're that agent. Answer their questions definitively and give them on-point, understandable information.

Be positive. You're asking the customer to make a very important financial decision over the phone, so he or she will naturally be hesitant. Give the customer time to work through his or her thoughts. Remain helpful and keep a good attitude. The second you turn hostile or even act impatient, the customer will put up his or her defenses, too.

Don't get distracted. Don't use speakerphone. Don't eat or drink or chew gum when you're on the phone. Don't watch the baseball game or try to talk to someone else in the office. Don't surf the Web or work on something else on your computer. The only thing you should do while you talk on the phone to a customer is take notes on the call. If you're not interested in the conversation, the customer will notice and think, "You don't care at all about me."

Stay on the line. You called the customer. So putting him or her on hold or cutting the conversation short sends a mixed message. You care enough to call, but not enough to actually devote some time to the conversation. It makes it look like you're only interested in the sale, wastes the customer's time and sends the implied message that you think your time is more important than his or hers.

Call at the right time. Be aware of the time zone the customer lives in, and whether your call may be coming too early or too late in the day. Customers who get calls, say, in the middle of dinner or before they wake up in the morning aren't going to want to hear what you have to say, no matter how cheerful and informative you are.

But what about when the customer calls you? Is that different from when you make the call yourself? There are a few things you can do to prepare yourself for a customer's call:

Keep your notes within reach. You don't want to be caught off-guard when a customer calls and be without your notes from the previous call. Always keep your notepad or digital notes handy so you can start right where you left off and you can take more notes on your continuing discussion. Ideally, you could keep your notes organized through a lead management system and have them available to bring up at a moment's notice.

Stay professional. A customer could call you at any time seeking an insurance quote. Even if you're in the middle of a stressful assignment or taking a coffee break, you want to come across as ready to do business when a customer calls. If you can't present a professional demeanor, don't answer. You'll lose the customer's business. Instead, let the call go to your voicemail and call the customer when you are more collected.

Let the customer drive the conversation and listen. There was a reason the customer picked up the phone to call you. Let the customer tell you exactly what his or her interest is and why he or she took the time to make the call. The customer may not have a perfect idea of what he or she is looking for, but you can tell from what is said exactly which direction you need to go. Then you can take the reins and tell the customer what you can offer and how it will fulfill his needs.

Have a genuine person-to-person talk. It's important you remain professional, but it's fine to have a talk with the customer about something you both enjoy – maybe sports or a shared interest in cars. It will loosen the customer up and make things smoother.

Make sure they understand the basics. The customer is calling you for a quote. Before you can provide one, you should make sure they understand what factors affected the price and how the policy works – generally what it covers and what it doesn't. That way the customer better understands what they're paying for, and will be more inclined to close the sale.

If you call a customer to find he or she doesn't pick up, don't get intimidated by the sound of the tone on his or her voicemail. Leave a message! It's a good way to let the customer know that you made an effort to make contact fast. Here are some things you can to do make your voicemail messages more effective:

Include your info. Leave a message that includes your name, agency, the reason for your call and your phone number. Ideally, give your phone number right away so that, if for some reason the customer doesn't get to the end of your message, he or she will have heard it.

Use your hook. Give them a reason to return your call. Customers are more likely to call back if you say you can help them use insurance to protect their financial security and livelihoods, rather than just, "I sell insurance, please call me back."

Don't give the quote in the message. It reduces your sale to a price tag, without telling the customer the features of the product. And even if you are sure the price is the lowest around, it still doesn't do you or the customer much of a service to reduce the conversation to one entirely about price.

Relax. A customer can hear when someone is nervous. And if you sound nervous, you may give the impression that you're not being completely honest or that you're just not confident in what you're selling.

Keep it short. Get all of the critical information in a short, clear, 20-second message (or even shorter, if you can manage it). Long messages are just begging to be skipped or deleted immediately.

Don't make it easy for customers to ignore you. Forgetting to repeat your number, speaking too quickly, sounding uninterested, or saying that you will call again are all reasons the potential customer can use to ignore your message and not return the call. Simply state your number and that you'd like the customer to call you back.

Watch your timing. The best hours to leave a voicemail message are between 6:45 AM to 8 AM and from 4:30 PM to 6:30 PM. The consumer may think of you as determined and won't be so quick to dismiss you.

Mix it up. Create several (about three to five) different and concise voicemail message scripts, if you decide to use a script. Alternate among them so that you can use them repeatedly but still sound fresh.

Here are some special tips and tricks used by top agents to sound better on the phone. Follow these and you will likely find your conversations going more smoothly.

Smile while you talk. Believe it or not, a smile can be heard over the phone. Your voice will sound more genuine and welcoming. This seemingly small action is subtle, yet results in customers being more inclined to like you and listen to what you have to say.

Stand up. If you want to come across as dynamic and compelling, stand up during your call. You automatically express more enthusiasm, energy and clarity in your voice when standing with good posture.

Use your customer's name. People like to hear their name, and they like to know that you care enough about them to remember it. If you want to keep a customer's attention from drifting, and keep them more involved in what you are saying, use their first name at least a few times during the phone call.

Add some "uh-huhs." It may sound silly, but responding to a customer with a simple "uh-huh" instead of dead silence shows the customer that you are listening while allowing them to continue what they are saying.

Don't let a "no" derail the conversation. People are practically programmed to say "no" or give a negative response to salespeople until they've been convinced that the salesperson actually has something worth their time. It's your job to try to overcome these negative responses. You don't need a firm "yes," just a maybe or some other sign of permission to continue with your conversation.

Talk like the customer does. When the customer is talking, listen to what kind of language they use, particularly adjectives; then speak in a similar manner without imitating the customer's voice. If the customer thinks you talk like he or she does, he or she will tend to feel you are more relatable.

Know what the competition's selling. It's good to be able to compare what you're selling with what you're competitors are selling, so you can list all the ways your product is superior.

Show how your policy fits in the customer's budget. If the customer insists he or she can't afford the policy, go through how you can help make it fit, from altering the policy.

End on a high note. Even if the customer decides to wait or turns you down altogether, remain polite and finish the conversation pleasantly. Though the person you just spoke to may not be your customer now, he or she may recommend you to others or come back to you at a later time.

Text messages work. Another phone-based approach you may want to consider is using text messaging to contact leads. According to the Direct Marketing Association, 70 percent of people respond to text messages, and 77 percent of people with cell phones use text messaging services. If nothing else, a text can be a good way to get a customer to give you a call and start talking about his or her quote.

It's a low-cost, easy way to make contact with potential customers or current customers. And it's yet another way you can make connections with people, another tool to add to your toolbox.[27]

Using E-mail

E-mail is a good and unobtrusive way to send information to clients and follow up after your initial phone or in-person conversation.

It's crucial that you send an email to every lead you purchase, and you are going to want to automate as much of this process as possible. Take the time to put together a thoughtful, well-worded email template to use. Here are some tips:

Much like with phone calls, you should **be warm and polite** in your message. Don't demand anything, just politely ask for a return e-mail if the customer has any interest whatsoever in the product you're offering.

Get to the point. Big blocks of text in e-mails make them hard to read. The customer could just

---

[27] Found at
http://www.insuremeblog.com/agent/2010/02/text-messaging-the-perfect-solution-to-lead-communication/.

delete it or move on to the next message in his or her inbox if there's too much to parse.

Include info about your agency. Include your phone number and address. Maybe even include a short paragraph about the background of your agency in your signature. The more open you are, the better.

Let the client know you will be calling them at some time in the near future. This is so you don't catch him or her off guard when you do call, and that he or she should be on the lookout for it.

Check and re-check your email for grammatical and spelling errors. A badly written e-mail looks terribly unprofessional.

Use a standard font like Arial or Times New Roman. Do not use custom fonts. Do not use Comic Sans, and do not use odd coloring choices or backgrounds that make your message hard to read. These mistakes will make you come across as unprofessional as well. Plus, the harder it is to read an e-mail, the less likely a customer is going to spend any time on it.[28]

Most importantly, don't think of your e-mail as a one-way message delivery system. If a customer replies to your e-mail message with questions, concerns or a request to meet or talk over the phone,

---

[28] Found at http://jerz.setonhill.edu/writing/etext/e-mail.htm.

reply in a courteous, conversational but professional way. Be prompt, and check your e-mail regularly to make sure you don't strike the customer as unresponsive.

Meeting In Person

Chances are you can achieve the most with your customers through in-person, face-to-face meetings where you can really get to know them and give them a chance to get to know you as well. It's not always possible to meet customers in person for all your discussions, but it's a good idea to meet face-to-face when you can, because it's amazing how much more you and your customer can gain from being in the same room and talking to one another.

Many of the communication techniques for using the phone – proving you're an expert, starting the conversation strong, ending on a good note – work just as well in person. But the advantage of the in-person meeting that you don't get over the phone or by e-mail is the ability to read the customer's body language.

Nearly three-fourths of all communication is non-verbal. So if you can learn signs to look for in a customer's body language, you can get a good idea about how he or she feels about your product and how you're presenting it, even if he or she isn't saying very much or – more likely – is saying things he or she doesn't mean just to bring the discussion to a conflict-free close. Odds are you've made that same maneuver yourself – maybe telling a persistent sales person at a clothing store you were just looking or a person trying to tell you something on the street that you were too busy to talk.

Learning how to understand when a customer is using those tactics – and finding out what they really mean by reading his or her non-verbal cues – can help you steer the conversation to your and the customer's advantage. And it shouldn't be too hard. Everyone is equipped with the basic tools needed to perceive what people are saying through what they're not saying.

But remember: Unless you've taken classes in reading body language, you're not an expert. Some of the smaller subtleties of what people say with their actions require professional training to really figure out. For your purposes, it's best to look at the broad, general gestures and get an impression of what the customer's feeling. You should also note that some customers may just be nervous people – meeting a new agent to talk about a major financial decision can put some butterflies in someone's stomach, obviously – so not every bad sign might mean the person is totally uncomfortable with your agency or the policy you're discussing. The discomfort could come from the situation itself.

Here are some things to look for to know that customers are receptive to what you're saying:

- Eye contact. If the client keeps looking right at you, that's a sign of comfort and confidence.
- A smile.
- The customer is leaning forward.
- A relaxed sitting position.
- Uncrossed arms, either resting on the arms of the chair or by his/her sides.
- Little to no movement or fidgeting.

And here's a list of things that might indicate that a customer isn't on the same track as you are:

- The client isn't making eye contact. This could indicate a lack of comfort or that the client isn't telling the truth and is perhaps just trying to escape the situation.
- Fidgeting. If the client's moving around a lot in his or her chair, that's not a sign of comfort. It's a sign of being very tense and not being able to settle in.
- Crossed arms. That's a defensive, closed position that means the client is not particularly receptive.

- Holding a drink or some other item at chest level is also closed body language.

- Leg shaking. It's a display of nervousness and discomfort.

- Rounded shoulders/bad posture. The customer is bored.[29]

If you know what to look for, you can let the customer know you understand what he or she is feeling, and ask what would make his or her experience better. That's something you can only do in a face-to-face discussion with a client.

---

[29] Found at http://www.selfgrowth.com/articles/kyle.html.

Chapter 8:

Staying in Touch

Your initial contact with a customer – be it over the phone, by e-mail or in person – is a very important part of the sales process, but it's not the only step. Whether your customer buys a policy after that first conversation or asks for more time to think, following up with calls, e-mails, meetings, and discussions on social media sites is another necessary step.

But it's worthless to just call up a customer or send an e-mail that simply reminds the customer you sell insurance and that asks if they remember when you talked. You need to deliver value each time you get back in touch with a customer. Calling just to check in or to make sure the customer got your last call or email is a bad idea. It doesn't tell the customer anything. It's just pestering. You need to a compelling reason for the call, such as an important update about their quote, something you forgot to mention before, or a great success story from another client you feel applies to your earlier conversations. Find a reason to follow up, then touch base.

On that same note, it's a good idea to keep your follow ups short and professional so that you don't bore the client. A good way to do this is to pay close attention to what your clients are saying and use your notes to your advantage as you go.

To make your follow ups smoother, be sure to create a bridge between your conversations. It's crucial to take notes when talking to customers and to take a few seconds to review those notes before you call them for a follow up. For instance, you could start the conversation by saying, "Last time we talked...," showing that you took the time to pay attention, take notes, and think about them is critical to building a long-term relationship with a new customer.

There are lots of reasons why it's important to take notes. For example, you make a follow-up call and ask the prospect, an older woman, if she had the chance to talk over the policy with her husband, only to be reminded that she already told you on the first call that her husband passed away 6 months ago. You can kiss that sale goodbye. In another example, the prospect has to re-explain everything he told you on the first call because you keep getting all the details wrong in your recollection. Say goodbye to that sale too.

Remember not to go overboard with your follow-ups. Wait at least a few days between each follow up call. That way, you keep yourself on the customer's mind without being a nuisance.

Sometimes agents will use e-mail templates for their follow-ups with customers. That's fine, but the most successful agents always personalize the e-mails they send. Leave an area at the top of your template to include some personal information about your client and a recap of the last time you talked. A personalized message will make any e-mail more worthwhile to a customer.[30]

But personalized messages aren't all you should be sending – e-mail newsletters you send to every client who agrees to it, and even some of your industry colleagues, can really get people involved in your agency, and make them feel like they're a part of your team. Your newsletter can also let customers know about new offers and initiatives that may benefit them and bring them into your office for a re-evaluation of their policies. These newsletters can be a good way to get information out to a lot of interested parties including customers, peers, local business leaders and others.

---

[30] Found at
http://smallbusinessonlinecommunity.bankofamerica.com/thread/26521.

As part of the e-mails, it's a smart move to send your clients some helpful links to websites that can answer all their questions regarding their policies, insurance in general and how they can do what's best for their finances and their families. Not only will those links help them make better decisions, they'll show that you're interested in more than just selling them something else.

It also is a good idea to do some direct mailings for follow-ups so that customers can be reminded that you're there for them – especially when the client's x-date is approaching. Brochures and postcards do a good job of letting customers know you care and you remember them – without seeming too intrusive.

More About Newsletters

Your monthly e-mail newsletter will let clients and colleagues know what you're doing, what you care about and what's going on in the larger insurance world, if you craft it the right way. It will be a very good way to let customers and others know that as an agent you're not just interested in taking their checks to the bank; you not only have an interest in your industry, but also in hobbies outside of it, and you want to share that information with the people you serve and with whom you work.

What should you put in your newsletter to make sure it comes across as what you mean it to – a gesture to provide helpful information, remind your customers and colleagues of your agency and a way to help them get to know you better? Here are some ideas:

- Include updates for anything new or exciting going on at your agency. Don't brag and don't get too into industry jargon here; just tell customers what new things you have to offer them, and how those products or services might benefit them and others.

- Write a personal message. Include a message with your picture directly from you that can add a little bit of a personal touch to your newsletter. Write about something you find fun or enjoyable in your everyday life, maybe sports or cars or cooking. Make sure what you write is inoffensive, but also shows a little bit of your personality.

- Include links to interesting or helpful articles. These could be articles about the insurance industry as a whole, ways to live a healthier lifestyle, car care tips, financial tips, and whatever else you think might be of interest to your customers.

- Use your agency logo.

- Include links to your agency's Facebook page, Twitter account, blog, website or any online tool customers might be able to use.

- Add a section focusing on specific customers in your agency. Give some quick profile information for customers who'd like to be featured. It will give your customers a feeling that they're really being recognized and that you care about them as human beings.

- If someone asks to be removed from your e-mail list, remove him or her. It doesn't do you any good to keep sending your newsletter to someone who doesn't want it.[31]

Keeping In Touch Via Social Networking

We've already discussed how you can use social networking to gain leads, grow your brand and network with other agents. But you can also use social networking sites, much like e-mail, to send messages to clients and potential clients.

Both Facebook and LinkedIn have messaging systems that allow you to send one person or a group a message much like an e-mail. Likewise, on Facebook you can write what's called a "note," a long-form

---

[31] Found at http://www.annuity-lead.com/2009/03/06/insurance-newsletter-has-prospects-call-you/.

message you can make visible to all your friends or fans. In those messages, you can generally promote new goings-on at your agency, tout features of the policies you sell or announce new initiatives. On the other hand, you can also send private messages to your friends/fans specifically geared toward them and looking at their personal needs and requirements.

On Twitter, you have the option of sending someone who follows you a "private message," which holds to the same 140-character limit but is only visible to the person to whom you send it. Likewise, you can carry on conversations with specific people by using the @ symbol in the regular Twitter timeline.[32]

The most apparent benefit of using social media sites to keep in contact with customers is that you'll be speaking to them, essentially, where they live. If you can make it acceptable to your customers to talk to them in their personal social media space, you'll have made yourself as much a part of their lives as their friends.[33] Your messages about expiration dates and new offers will be right in the mix with wedding announcements and party invitations. You can become

---

[32] Found at

http://blog.junta42.com/content_marketing_blog/2009/06/42-online-content-sharing-and-productivity-tools.html.
[33] Found at http://mashable.com/2009/10/28/small-business-marketing.

as much a part of a customer's life as those other events.

Your Company Blog

The blog you set up for your agency can be a great tool for staying in touch with customers in a way that doesn't make them feel like you're constantly tapping them on the shoulder or otherwise bothering them to tell them about your agency. It lets them read about what's going on with you and your agency on their own time.

Like your newsletter, you can use your blog to post news and updates about your agency, but also to show a little of your own personality and hobbies. Don't be afraid to write something that isn't necessarily entirely about your agency, the insurance you sell or insurance at all. Just make it worth reading and of interest to the customers you send to the blog.

Some other things to keep in mind:

- You should secure a domain name/title for your business blog immediately, whether you use it or not. This keeps competitors from snatching up or, even worse, using your name.

- Don't spread yourself too thin. If you have the resources to create a blog from the ground up, great, but if you don't there are plenty of places such as Wordpress.com, Blogger.com and Posterous where you can start a ready-made blog from a template.

- Write great, focused content about your agency and industry. The better the content, the faster your audience will grow. It doesn't have to be novel quality, it just has to be something you think is interesting and you feel other people will find interesting, too.

- Make it easy to promote. Include buttons that allow users to link your posts on Facebook, Twitter and LinkedIn. You can find buttons on those specific websites to post on your blog and direct people to your other pages. But don't clutter up the page too much; keep it relatively simple to use.

Video

Another valuable thing you might want to include in your blog or anywhere in your agency's online presence is video. Videos are a cheap an effective way to add some personality to your brand and put a human face on your message. High-definition cameras for web videos are relatively inexpensive (such as the Flip), as is basic editing software. It's worth the expense, as more and more users on the Web are now coming to sites for more than just pictures and text; they want to see helpful videos as well.

Using video is a good way to get involved in the online conversation with someone's real voice. It also gives your customers and others the opportunity to chime in with their own videos whenever they please.

E-mail Integration

For years, marketers have looked for ways to use e-mail as a way to spread their messages to huge networks of people through forwarding. Social media has made that easier through the use of their own e-mail-like systems, the use of blogs and basic communication between networks.

Many social media sites now offer buttons for content creators to place either in e-mails, blog posts or their own websites so that readers might share that information with others in their networks. But allowing users to share information you send them doesn't mean it will necessarily happen. You have to make them want to share it.[34]

You should also try your best to make things you write, especially on your blog, go "viral." The key to success in e-mail and social network marketing is to

---

[34] Found at
http://c0180741.cdn.cloudfiles.rackspacecloud.com/pdf/sm-wp-socialmedia.pdf.

make the audience you initially market to into marketers themselves. How do you do that? Offer them a reward for sending a coupon to their friends, for instance. Give them value for giving others value. From that starting point, the message will be sent to more and more people as the invitees become the inviters. For instance, you offer the people to whom you send an initial e-mail a $15 discount on some new product if they forward an e-mail offering a fee waiver to first-time customers at your agency.

And finally, know your audience. Make sure what you're offering to people through e-mail or through a social media site is something they want and something they'd want to share. And make it fun for them! Nobody wants a dry, unfriendly ad filling up his or her mailbox. Give your clients a reason to read your e-mails, either through a laugh or something that can turn into a fun game between them and their friends.

Chapter 9:

Recognizing Your Customers as People, Not Numbers

Now more than ever it's important that you get to know your customers as people with real interests, real personalities and real concerns rather than just another potential sale, a revenue boost for your agency or a policy number with an expiration date. That may sound like common sense or simple lip service to the old "customer's always right" cliché, but with the advent of social media, with posts on Yelp and other sites going out to the world about your agency, your customers have more say now in how people perceive your business than they ever have before. If customers believe that you see them as nothing more than faceless cogs in a machine to bring you more money, they'll say so where lots of people will be able to read it, and you'll lose trust.[35]

---

[35] Information on customer relationship management found at: http://www.destinationcrm.com/Articles/CRM-News/Daily-News/What-Is-CRM-46033.aspx.

You don't want that kind of bad word-of-mouth out there on the Internet about you, where nothing, even if it's deleted, is ever totally gone.[36]

So let's start with some quick tips for how to make sure your customers feel appreciated:

- **Be honest.** Sounds simple, right? But that doesn't just mean you shouldn't tell outright lies. Though, of course, you shouldn't. You should avoid half-truths and embellishments, too. Overpromising your agency's capabilities will always backfire. Simply be confident in the product you're selling, and present it as it really is, with both the pros and the cons. You know you have a great product, so with proof of your excellent customer service, you won't need to tell the customer anything more than the truth.

- **Don't just pretend to care.** Your customers are smart. They can tell when someone is just feigning interest in their concerns and needs. If you don't seem to care about what the customer wants, that customer will simply find someone who does.

---

[36] More on online CRM at http://www.destinationcrm.com/Articles/Editorial/Magazine-Features/Who-Owns-the-Social-Customer-54028.aspx.

- **Listen.** When you prove to a customer that you've really been hearing what he or she is saying either by asking an insightful question or simply trying to incorporate all of the customer's needs into his or her policy, you'll prove you're the right agent.

- **Remember it's not a game.** Don't play your conversation like it is one. This is the customer's real life. To them, this isn't about winning or losing a sale. It's about financial and personal security.

- **Be open.** A real conversation shouldn't be one-sided. So open up to your clients and tell them about your own experiences to illustrate how you understand their specific situations. Maybe you could tell an anecdote about another similar client or about when you personally had to make a decision like the one you're making now. Talk about your family, your kids, your commute to work that morning. Disclosing your own personal experiences will lead your clients to open up, too.

- **Prove that others trust you.** You could do this through using testimonials from other satisfied customers or displaying credentials from a trade group.

- **Prove that you trust yourself.** If you don't show confidence in your product and yourself, your customer won't have any reason to be confident in you. So don't question yourself in front of the customer, don't stumble over your words and, as the old cliché goes, don't let them see you sweat.

You also want to make sure you don't seem gimmicky or come across as a huckster. Your customers are smart and they can tell pretty quickly when someone's putting on a façade. The more genuine you are in your presentation, the more your customer is likely to respect and feel comfortable around you. Consider some ways you can prove your authenticity:

Know what you're selling. You're the expert. Your customer will come into your office with an expectation that you'll know the answers to their questions and how to best craft a policy to fit their needs. Don't give them a reason to think otherwise. Demonstrate your knowledge of every nook and cranny of that policy.

Make things understandable. As we mentioned before, one of the easiest ways to scare off a customer is to speak in an insider language he or she doesn't understand.

Get to know the customer. Trying to fit every person who comes into your office into a few pre-set policies is a good way to lose business. People aren't machines; everyone is different and has different needs. Don't ever use a cookie-cutter approach. If the customer's willing to talk about his or her family, listen to what he or she says about them. Learn their names. Ask about the customer's kids next time they come in. Find out what the customer's hobbies are, what he or she likes to do, what's important in his or her life right now. A little can go a long way.

Focus on the broad concepts and benefits. Don't get bogged down in numbers and figures. Outside of the price and coverage levels, your customers probably don't have any interest in all the various figures you have showing the effectiveness of the policy. The customer wants to know the long-term benefit of your product. Show it to him or her in a demonstrable way – through anecdotes or scenarios.

Demonstrate your real enthusiasm. If you're not excited about your product, why should anyone else be? Let the customer know upfront that you like the product you're selling and can't wait to tell him or her all about it. And don't frame it as a sales pitch. Really tell the customer why you got into the insurance business to sell the policies you're selling. If the customer can see you're a believer in your product and what you can do for people, you can make him or her a believer, too.[37]

To go into a little more detail, here are some things you can do through the process of your sales presentation to make things go smoother for both you and the client.

First off, don't sell the product over the phone unless you have to. Wait for the in-person meeting if you can. Ask your client would be interested in saving their household or business a lot of money, and that you can tell them how in just 10 minutes. It's hard to turn down saving money.

In the first moments of the conversation, the biggest hurdle to clear is the anxiety and nervousness your customer is likely feeling speaking to an insurance agent he or she has never met before. Try to start with some small talk. Before you get into the details of the policy you're selling or what the customer is looking for, ask what's going on in his or her life. What else is on the client's mind? Getting it off of his or her chest is a good way to keep a worry from distracting the customer later on. Plus, you could offer up some advice from personal experience to ease the client's mind and show you care about him or her as a person.

---

[37] The Million Dollar Round Table Center for Productivity. *Million Dollar Selling Techniques.* 1999, pp. 90-93.

One way to cut out those anxieties is to ask for a decision, not a sale. Tell the client first thing that you're not asking them to buy anything right away. You just want him or her to let you know whether the policy you describe fits his or her needs and to keep an open mind. They'll be receptive to what you offer, and will know that money isn't your only concern.

Then ask your client what he or she is looking for. What would you want an insurance policy to do for you? How much would you be willing to pay? Set an achievable bar early on. Then, you can show the client just how your products go over the bar the client his or herself has set.

Next, focus on the biggest priorities the client sets out. Focus on the two or three major points in the policy you're offering that you think will be most important to the client. The old rule is that 90 percent of your sale will be based on 10 percent of the features you offer. Discuss the other parts of the policy as well, but don't spend too much time on them.

Every time you hit a major point in your presentation, ask the client, "Would you be interested in that?" or "Is that what you were looking for?" You'll get an idea of what's important to the customer, so you can continue to focus on that feature. You might even get the client to agree to buy the policy right then and there.

It might also be useful to ask the client to take your place for just a second. If he or she was trying to convince you to try to buy a product he or she really believed in, what would they say? What would he or she change about the product? What questions would the client ask? This is a way to get the client to tell you what's stopping him or her from moving forward with buying the policy.

And remember: Don't bring up the price until you absolutely have to. Once the price enters the conversation, that will be the only thing that matters anymore. But you know and your customer knows that price isn't the only worthwhile part of the policy. If your customer asks, "How much?" tell him or her that you want to get through the main points and you can talk about price at the end. Or simply ask, "Is price the only important aspect of the policy for you?" Odds are, they'll say "no," and you can progress through the main points.

As your conversation with the client winds down, there are several things you can do to get your clients to decide whether buying your policy is the right thing for them so you can avoid indecision or an unwanted objection to what you're offering.

For instance, you could do some of the legwork for your customer and list the pros and cons. An indecisive client may not be thinking rationally about what the benefits and the setbacks of the policy you're selling are. So help them. Draw a line down a piece of paper and ask the client to list the pros and cons of buying the policy.

You could also use an anecdote about a client who was in a similar position and couldn't make up his or her mind. Describe how that client made the right decision, bought the policy and how that has improved that client's life.

And remember these things through the entirety of your conversation so that your customer remains comfortable and feels like you're invested in the discussion.

Be attentive. If you're distracted – constantly glancing at your phone or your computer screen, asking the customer to hold on a second while you talk to others in your office, or you simply zone out – your client will get frustrated and question whether you really have any interest in helping him or her. Maintain eye contact, stay involved in the conversation and don't let anything else grab your attention.

Call the client by name and talk to him or her in a conversational way, not a stilted way. In that same vein, stay relaxed. If you're high-strung, you'll just give the client a reason to be on edge, too.

And be sure to let the customer say his or her piece. If your client expresses hesitation about a specific detail of a policy or has a point to make, open the floor up to him or her. Once the client has voiced the issue, he or she will feel better to have gotten it out and you can know just what concerns you need to alleviate.

As for what you say, pay close attention to it. You can come across one of three ways: A nervous introvert who lacks confidence, a huckster who just wants the customer's money or a calm, confident agent who understands insurance and the customer. Obviously, you'll want to be the latter.

But how will you know that what you're saying comes across that way?

First, **listen to yourself.** Maybe record what you say and listen to it. Are there any awkward phrases? Things you could have said better? Things that sound fake, insincere? Do you hear nervousness or fidgeting in your voice? If you can catch those things, you can improve them.

Don't say things like "to tell you the truth" and "I'll try." Any time you start a sentence assuring the customer you're being honest, it puts a question in his or her head. Have you not been honest up to now? It sure sounds like it. And if you're constantly telling customers you'll try to do things – you'll try to get something to them by a certain date or you'll try to get a particular detail into their policy – tells them that you might not be able to do it, or that you plan not to, but just aren't willing to say so. If you can do it, say you can. If you can't, say that. They'll appreciate your honesty.

Eliminate conflict. Certain words – "but," "disagree," "can't" – are dismissive and combative. Avoid using them. Instead, use "and," "understand" and "could" to show that you see where your client is coming from, however, you wish to offer an alternative view and another path to the same goal.

Don't place limits on yourself. Words like "only" and "just" restrict what you have done and what you plan to do. They belittle you and they belittle the product. If you speak without those words, your statements will be a lot stronger. The exception, of course, is when you want to minimize something, like, say, the price of the policy you're offering.

Try not to sound to obligated or burdened. Phrases like "I'll have to" or "find the time" make it seem like your meeting with the client is something you're not particularly interested in. It shows that you don't really like your job and would prefer to be doing something else. Saying that you'll be "glad" to do things for clients or that it would be "my pleasure" shows you're ready to and willing to do the work. Try to use those instead.[38]

And finally, **always be sure to end on a good note.** If the customer opts to not buy a policy that day, stay polite and try to close out the conversation on a positive. Maybe circle back around to your earlier small talk or wishing the customer good luck in whatever's going on in his or her life. Sounding irritated or hanging up on them is a guaranteed way to never hear from the customer again. You never know if they will tell friends that you were rude. Word-of-mouth spreads pretty fast, especially now with sites like Yelp and Facebook.

The key to a good reputation is simply being an agent people like. So be likeable! If you have a quality product to sell, there's really not much more to it than that. But remember: How you deal with customers in your office and over the phone is now a major component of how you market yourself. Every meeting is a marketing opportunity. Be your best!

---

[38] The Million Dollar Round Table Center for Productivity, *Million Dollar Closing Techniques*. 1999, pp. 191-200.

Chapter 10:

Overcoming Objections

One of the best ways to let customers know that you really do care about their concerns is to address their objections in ways other than just to dismiss them. Alleviate the problem, and you can progress.

Lots of times, agents will hear an objection like "I need more time to think," "Let me talk to my wife/husband," or "I just can't afford it" as an out-and-out "no." But that's not really what they are, most of the time. They're more like a request for help. The customer wants to know how he or she can afford the policy, needs to clarify how this is good for his or her family and is looking for the right sign of confirmation that this is, in fact, the best policy.[39]

And sometimes customers have suspicions about the industry, specific companies within the insurance industry, and the cost of the policy versus

---

[39] Found at http://www.dirjournal.com/guides/sales-objections-are-sales-opportunities/.

the hassle and insurance agents in general. Maybe they've been burned in the past, or heard horror stories from friends and family about an expensive policy that ended up covering nothing.

Plus, often customers are shopping for insurance during times of pretty intense uncertainty in their lives. Maybe they just moved, lost their job or had to deal with the illness of a loved one, prompting them to get coverage or change it. Or possibly they just made a big investment – a house, a car, a boat or a business. It's understandable that your customers may be a little more on-edge and confused at this point in their lives.

So how do you alleviate those fears? Talk it out. Make them trust you. And show your customer you really appreciate him or her, as we advocated in the previous chapter.

Ask your customer what he or she is looking for. A low rate? A local agent? Just to compare rates? Or something in the coverage he or she hasn't gotten before? Once you have an idea of what the customer's chief priority is, you can craft your presentation with a focus on that topic. That way, you can avoid the customer's later objections altogether. Any question the customer may have, you'll know it upfront, and you can deal with it.[40]

---

[40] Found at http://www.chrisg.com/overcoming-sales-objections/.

But in the event that a customer still harbors an objection once you've finished up your presentation, here are some things to keep in mind:

- **Avoid lectures.** The last thing a person wants to hear when they're trying to buy insurance or anything else is a list of reasons why they're wrong. It's fine to gently guide customers into the right direction, but if you start finger wagging or talking about mistakes customers made in the past, they'll just feel bad and want to get away from you.

- **Get them to explain the objection.** If someone says, "I can't afford it," ask what you need to do so they can afford it. Or simply rephrase what the customer said as a question: "You say you can't afford it?" That will get the customer talking and you can hash out some ways to get past the perceived problem.

- **Don't get bogged down in details and jargon.** Just because some words and phrases mean a lot to you as an insurance agent, that doesn't mean they mean anything to your customers. The smallest details of a policy or the industry conventional wisdom about why a policy is good won't do anything for your customer – he or she just wants to know why this policy is right for his or her life. Remember that and don't do anything that will confuse him or her.

- **Avoid assumptions.** You may think you know the reason why a customer says he or she needs more time or will have to consult another family member. But you don't. There could be any number of reasons a customer tells you those things. If you believe it's just an excuse, you'd better be sure before you give up on the sale.

- **Know the best responses.** If one of your responses to a common objection works well, remember it. Write it down. Use it the next time that objection comes up, with the understanding that not every customer is cut from the same cloth. They may use the same objection, but they may not mean the same thing or have the same reasons.

- **Never react negatively.** If you get angry or start telling customers things like, "But you could save so much money!" or "But I haven't finished describing it yet," you have squandered your chance. Stay calm, stay focused and keep your eye on your goal of making sure the customer is satisfied and confident in you.[41]

- **Don't get defensive and don't take it personally.** This isn't about you; it's about the customer and you being able to convince him or her of the value of your product. Simply reiterate the value of what you're selling and don't feel like you have to defend your integrity or professionalism. And make sure you don't badmouth a competitor or another insurance company if the customer brings one up; it makes you look petty and doesn't help your cause.

So what are you most likely to hear from customers when an objection does rise? In our experience from years in the insurance industry and based on what we hear from the hundreds of agents we work with, the following dozen or so statements are the ones you're most likely to hear.

First, and possibly most common, "I can't afford it."

Sometimes, this is just the truth. A customer comes into an insurance agent's office expecting to

---

[41] Found at
http://www.sellingandpersuasiontechniques.com/overcoming-sales-objections.html.

hear one thing, and they end up hearing a number much higher than they thought, and, after crunching some numbers in his or her head, decides it's just not in his or her budget. In those cases, there's not much you can do.

But those instances are the exception. Most of the time, the customer believes he or she can't afford the policy because you haven't demonstrated its value. So it's up to you to really prove that the product you're selling is worth the cost. That might mean going through all the different benefits of coverage or telling a story about a customer whose financial security was saved through having insurance.

Shift the conversation away from one regarding price. Make it about how other customers who also thought they couldn't afford the policy ended up buying one – and how much good it did for them. Make it about how you can accommodate the customer with payment plans or by changing the policy. There are ways to make it work.

Next: "I need to think it over and get back to you."

The easy response to this one is to ask the client what he or she is thinking about. Maybe you can help him or her think it through. Maybe what the customer really needs is some more explanation, and the reason he or she needs to think something through is because something about the policy wasn't made completely clear.

This is a big decision for the customer. Make sure he or she knows that you're aware of that, and you want to do all you can to make this choice go smoothly for him or her. Tell the customer that you understand how important this is and you want to make sure they know everything possible to help him or her with the decision. The customer will appreciate it.

Another one you might hear is, "I'd like to shop around a little more."

This objection might mean that something the customer was looking for – a certain type of coverage or a price point – wasn't apparent in the initial policy you offered. Or it might mean that they're just unsure of what's available in the marketplace. Or it could be they're just feeling nervous and don't want to commit to buying the policy. Ask the customer what is driving him or her to check around, and see if you maybe you could help them knock out that curiosity then and there.

It's natural for customers to want to shop around. Just like you'd probably go to more than one store to check on prices for a dishwasher, customers want to know where to get the best deal. But you might be able to help the customer shop around right there in your office.

If you're an independent agent, you can be their "shopping around". You can show the customer prices from an assortment of providers, so be sure to let the customer know you have that capability.

For captive agents, it's a little tougher. But one thing you can do is tell the customer about the stability and reliability your agency can provide. Your association with a major provider gives you a backing you can't get with independent agencies. The price the customer pays provides them not only with a policy but also with the assurance of connecting with a company and an agency that will be there for the long haul. Tell the customer about your excellent customer service and how people on social networking sites have said great things about you. Show them testimonials. Use your reputation to your advantage.

A customer might ask you to e-mail or mail him or her some more information about your policy, your agency or the provider you work for. When that happens, you should ask the customer what they're missing and why you wouldn't be able to fill that gap right then and there. Clear it up as soon and as efficiently as you can.

What if your customer says he or she just wants to stick with his or her current policy? That raises the question of why the customer is talking to you to begin with. If the customer is completely satisfied with his or her policy, why would he or she be looking to anybody else, even just to talk?

Without saying anything negative about the customer's current provider, ask that customer why he or she decided to come talk to you that day or why he or she accepted your phone call. There had to be a reason. What spurred his or her interest? Is there a way you could help them figure out how to get what they're looking for?

Also, ask why the customer likes his or her current policy. What works? Is there a way that could work better? Jot down some notes and see if you can assess the client's situation.

And remind the customer that times change. If he or she has had the same policy for the past five or 10 years, things might be very different now than when the customer first signed that plan. It's possible the client's paying too much or has insufficient coverage. You should let them know if that's the case. It might be time to take a look at that old policy, go through it, and see if there are any big gaps in there.

Another thing you might consider is asking your customer a specific question about his or her current policy that would be very pertinent to his or her situation. The customer might immediately answer, "Yes, I have that," but it's also possible that he or she might say, "I don't know what that is. Should I have that?" This gets your customer to keep talking and may get him or her to be a little more receptive to what you're offering.

In the event that a customer protests that he or she has never heard of you or maybe doesn't trust you because you're not local, it's a sign that you have to prove that you're a trusted and well-respected agent. Maybe you could show that you're on Angie's List or another online source, or have a good reputation with the Better Business Bureau or local Chamber of Commerce. Maybe you could read a few of your Yelp reviews. Or you could mention that you're a member of a trade association such as PIA, Trusted Choice or NAIFA.

It could be that your customer is simply suspicious about insurance in general, or the specific company with which your agency is associated. Or they knew someone who got a raw deal from an insurance provider.

Find out exactly what the causes of the customer's reluctance and suspiciousness are. See if you can get detailed reasons for why the customer feels like an insurance agent or the insurance industry has wronged the customer his or herself or someone the customer knows. Does the customer know the whole story? Could it have been a simple misunderstanding?

Obviously, every industry's going to have some bad actors who do some things that make the honest people in those industries look bad. And insurance has been particularly plagued by that effect in recent years with companies like AIG taking the spotlight. Tell the customer you understand their suspicions and, hey, you'd be suspicious, too, after all that's happened in insurance over the past few years. But not everybody in the insurance industry is out to get people or act as moneygrubbers. You're certainly not one of them; you're a local agent who got into this business to help people in your community.

You can prove that through customer testimonials and good reviews you've gotten online. Along with an honest demeanor and a cheerful attitude, you should be able to help the customer get the bad taste out of his or her mouth.

Let's say you give a customer a presentation on a policy that would be perfect for his or her current situation. After a few moments of thought, the customer leans forward and says, "Now that I think about it, I don't think I even really need insurance. It's not really a priority and I've never really experienced a big loss that required it."

Ask why the customer thinks he or she doesn't need insurance, and listen closely to the reasons.

Then take the opportunity to tell the customer that, just because they've never needed insurance before, that doesn't mean they'll never need it. And if they had to deal with a terrible situation like a totaled car or a house fire, they'd be left out in the cold without any coverage. Would the customer have the money available to replace what he or she lost? Probably not. The cost of a premium would definitely be more palatable than having to replace items he or she has likely been paying off for years.

And even if no huge disaster comes – and one always hopes that such a thing never happens – isn't the peace of mind, knowing that the customer's financial security is protected, worth it?

There's also a chance that the customer could simply say he or she is too busy to go through the whole process right now or that it's not a good time for him or her to pay for a policy. It's easy to deal with that one. Ask what a good time in the near future would be, and make yourself available. And maybe even stress that it won't take any longer than just a few minutes to go through the process of getting him or her covered.

If the customer says he or she doesn't quite understand how the policy is going to do anything for them, or that they're just not interested, the answer again is to show the customer the value. As we said before, that's about making the customer's perception of what the policy is line up with the cost. And there's always the option of making changes to the policy to make have more value.

Another possible objection a customer could raise is that he or she needs to talk with his or her spouse, another family member, an advisor, a business partner or even an attorney before making a buying decision.

If the customer says he or she has to consult with a husband or wife, the best thing to do would be to ask if the customer will see or talk to his or her spouse that day. See if the two of them can arrange an appointment with you that evening or the next day where you can all sit down and talk about the pros and cons of the policy that best fits them. If that's not possible, maybe you could get them all on a conference call or an e-mail thread.

The same could apply for anybody else the customer feels a need to consult with. If you can get everybody into the office to talk it out, everyone will be better off, because nobody will be getting second-hand information. The customer's financial advisor can get a look at the policy right then and right there, and hear from you just what's involved.

If you're dealing with professional advisors or attorneys, remember that you're almost certainly going to get raked over the coals with legal questions and queries about loopholes or potential problems. Be prepared, don't dodge any questions and give confident answers. Just the facts.

And finally, your customer may simply let you know that he or she is uncomfortable, overwhelmed or being pulled in too many directions by agents who are trying to sell him or her a policy. The customer's not sure whom to trust.

You can probably relate to this. We've all been in situations where several people are asking for your time and attention and it's hard to know who to listen to. And in those situations, whom would you have likely ended up listening to? Probably the person you felt the best connection with. The one who seemed the most like you.

Be that person for your client. Tell him or her that you've been exactly where they're sitting, and you really could have benefited from someone walking you through the process of making the right decision. Offer to do that for him or her. Together, list the client's main objectives in buying insurance and chief concerns. What's most important to them? What could he or she live without? Get to the real values.

Then, go through a process of knocking out each concern with the policy you offer. Give the customer some options and get lots of input from him or her. Take it slowly and make sure the customer understands everything. Repeat things if you have to. Explain things in very basic terms. Don't assume the customer automatically knows what you're talking about.

This almost grade-school approach, along with your other efforts to let the customer know you're trustworthy and respected in the community, should ease the customer into believing that you are the agent they've been looking for, and make your voice stand out from the crowd of other agents vying for that customer's business.[42]

---

[42] The Million Dollar Round Table Center for Productivity, *Million Dollar Closing Techniques*. 1999, pp. 117-142.

140

Chapter 11:

Successfully Closing

Everything we've discussed so far – the changes in marketing, the ways to promote your agency, buying leads, the process of getting to know your customer as a person, dealing with objections – these are all steps toward your ultimate goal of closing sales and making your agency profitable. That's one thing that hasn't changed one bit.

As we said earlier, the process of selling insurance to a customer isn't a game or a competition – these are important moments in people's lives – and you shouldn't treat it as one. However, there are some techniques and strategies that can help you close a little more easily and get the customer to move forward with buying a policy that will ultimately help him or her secure a solid financial future.

Some of the basics are things we've already mentioned in previous chapters – completely knowing the ins-and-outs of what you're selling, making sure you avoid jargon and industry talk, establishing a relationship with your customer, focusing on the broad benefits rather than the minor details, and being highly enthusiastic about your product. [43]

But here are some techniques you can use to help things movie along in addition to those initial basics.

We've all heard the cliché that states what happens when you assume. Let's just say it's generally thought of as a mistake. But there's actually something to be gained from the assumption that your client will consent to buying the policy you offer to him or her. You're offering what you know to be a great product. So it should be relatively safe to assume that the customer would want it unless he or she says otherwise or expresses skepticism. You might close your discussion with the client by starting to fill out some paperwork. If the client doesn't stop you, the sale is made. The worst that can happen is the conversation continues for a little while until the client is more comfortable. It's pretty unlikely that a client is going to get up in arms over you just starting to fill out some papers.

---

[43] More at
http://www.evancarmichael.com/Sales/3193/The-5-Secrets-of-closing-the-sale.html.

But jumping right for the paperwork probably isn't your best move. That needs to come after you spend a little time easing the customer into the process. You need to take a piece-by-piece approach to work your way up to the final sale.

You'll want to do some preparation for yourself prior to meeting with the client. Set some goals for how you want the discussion to go and where you'd like it to end up, not only for you but also for your customer.

Obviously, you'll have your main goal of finally making the sale, but you should set smaller goals or benchmarks for yourself as you move along the way, in addition to the bigger-picture goals for where you'd like your agency to be a year, five years or 10 years from now. In his book, *10 Steps to Success*, Daniel S. Fowler sets out lots of areas where you should set goals for yourself, including your management strategy, budget, office setup and mission statement. Those are all great to have, both in the long-term and short-term.

Once you set those goals, keep up with how you're doing. Take some time every now and again to take stock of where you are in making a specific sale or growing your agency to where you want it to be. The more aware of where you are, the more likely you'll be to get where you hope to go.

A good way to keep up with where you are is to put each lead you have into a category within your lead management system. You can label your leads that are ready to close, for instance, as "ready," leads you've just entered as "new," current clients as "current," those that aren't ready yet as "working," invalid ones as "invalid," leads with no activity as "dormant," and those that are totally off your radar as "dead."[44]

This gives you a good idea of which leads to pursue further and lets you focus your efforts. Keep those categories regularly updated, prioritize your work and you'll see more closes because of a wiser use of your time. But even those prospects that have seemingly gone cold deserve some of your effort. Continue sending them e-mail newsletters and special offers.

But what about in the specific meeting you're having right now? What can you do there to put you in the direction of achieving your goals?

A good way to get the customer involved in the process and to avoid surprises – which are the last thing a customer wants in a sales situation, unless the surprise is something like a much lower rate than he or she expected – is to set an agenda and present it to the customer at the beginning of the conversation. That

[44] Found at http://blog.prospectzone.com/?p=44.

way, the customer knows what you'll be talking about, and in what order. The customer can let you know what you've left out or what topics on the agenda he or she doesn't really need to discuss. It helps save your time and the customer's to set a game plan ahead of time. It also makes you look professional, organized and predictable – in a good way. A customer likes to know what he or she can expect from an insurance agent. So get in the habit of using an agenda.

Once the agenda is set, try asking the client to make a small decision – maybe what kind of folder he or she wants the paperwork put in or if they'd like to use a notepad – to start the decision-making process along. Once the client makes a few minor decisions and he or she is used to making choices with you in the room, you can work up to larger decisions such as deductible amounts and ultimately buying the policy.[45]

A similar technique is to use what literary types call "synecdoche." In understandable terms, that means "using the part in place of the whole." At the end of your discussion, ask the client a question that seems small but that would really determine whether he or she is buying the policy. For instance, you could ask whether the client wants to pay monthly or annually, or maybe if they'd like to add someone else onto a homeowners policy. If the client answers the

---

[45] Found at http://www.businessbyphone.com/25.htm.

question without saying, "I'm not buying anything yet," that client has just given you a clue toward his or her answer.

You don't just have to wait for the conversation with the client to end, either, to get an idea of where things are going. You can try to gauge things as your discussion goes along to see if the customer's going to buy the policy. As your presentation progresses, ask the client a question to test if he or she is ready to close the sale. Something like, "Do you think what I just described is what you're looking for?" or "What do you think so far?" or maybe "Do you like what I described so far?"

Asking those questions accomplishes two goals. First, it gives you a way to see if the customer is ready to buy the policy. Second, you get an opportunity to find out if the customer has any reasons for not buying the policy and refute them. Just like when you're answering objections, you can lay out your reasons why those roadblocks aren't true. You can use that as a good summation to leading up to starting to fill out the paperwork.

At some point in the conversation, you're going to come to a moment of decision for the customer. At that moment, it's important you use some strategy to make sure the customer doesn't rush things and that you take every opportunity you can to close the sale.

For instance, using silence can play a big part in bringing the sale to a close. Let's say, for instance, that a customer may seem less than totally ready to make a decision about the policy and is likely to ask for more time to make a choice. Present the client with the paperwork you've already filled out, tell him or her to look it over and think about it, and then say nothing. Sit in silence for as long as it takes until the client states his or her decision to buy the policy, turn it down or definitely take more time to think it over. At the very least, you'll have given your client an opportunity to be alone with his or her thoughts and weigh out his or her decision.

It's also always good for a client to hear that he or she isn't the only customer you've had who's been in the same position. If you can tell the story of another customer – or even yourself in a similar situation – who had a tough time deciding but ended up getting a lot out of buying a policy tell it.

If your customer simply cannot commit to buying the policy – it's too expensive or he or she just can see the use for it -- and gets up to walk out of the office, it can't hurt to give it one last try. Once he or she stands up, odds are the client will start to breathe a little easier and drop some of his or her tension. Use this opportunity, as they grab the doorknob, to quickly ask the client what you could have done better. What you could have done to help them get to where they needed to be to sign up for the policy. Hopefully, the client will get two things out of that question: You're a sincere person who wants to do better, and a chance to rethink how the whole process went. Just maybe he or she will give you an answer that can start the conversation going again, allow you to explain something the customer didn't understand or that was off-putting and give you a chance to close.[46]

Once you finally close the sale, congratulate yourself. You did a great job! But remember: This is just the beginning. Closing is simply the climax of a process that extends well beyond the moment your client signs up for a policy.

From the point of purchase forward it's up to you to continue to offer your client the best customer service you can, as well as make yourself available to answer any questions or concerns. Likewise, it's up to you to use the momentum you gain from the close into gaining more customers and growing your book of business. Is the client you just sold a policy to obviously satisfied? Ask for a referral. Does he or she use social networking sites such as Twitter or Facebook? Ask the client to look you up. Would they be interested in your e-mail newsletter? Get the client's

---

[46] The Million Dollar Round Table Center for Productivity, *Million Dollar Closing Techniques*. 1999, pp. 47-93.

e-mail address. The follow-through is just as important as the swing.

And, of course, you should always follow up with customers when x-dates come around. You don't want to lose a customer just because you forgot to ask him or her to renew. Closing is undoubtedly the aspect of your agency that brings in the most revenue. But always remember that your customers – people, not documents or checks – are the real lifeblood of your business. Treat them well and they'll help your agency expand to the thriving business you want it to be.

Closing is the goal, but it's not everything. So much goes into gaining new customers and keeping those customers beyond simply making the sale. Don't let your focus get too narrow.

Chapter 12:

Best Practices

In the course of selling leads and working with agents all over the United States, we've had a lot of conversations about the best ways to use leads, run an agency and grow books of business.

You might be surprised to find out that some of the biggest-selling agents in the country are pretty open about what they think are the reasons they've been so successful. These aren't any trade secrets locked in a vault like the original Coca-Cola formula or anything like that. Agents, in general, are happy to provide their peers with tips for the best practices in selling insurance of all kinds.

Virtually all the agents we talk to who have seen a lot of success using leads to sell policies agree on one major point: You have to be the first agent to make contact with a customer.

On making contact first:

- Zachary Ebner of Farmers Insurance Group in Plano, Illinois: "If it's 15 minutes old, half an hour old, an hour old, you're pretty much already too late. Obviously, you have a chance if you let it go a little bit, but that means that the other insurance agencies have already called those people, and a) already given them a rate they like and go with it or b) already heard from so many insurance agents they just don't want to talk to you anymore." Also recommends sending an e-mail and making a phone call to try and contact the customer first.

- Cheryl Bowker of Bowker Insurance Agency in Livonia, Michigan: Her agents send an e-mail immediately to potential customers, then call within about 10 minutes. Her advice for what you should do if you don't get an answer on that first call is pretty simple: Keep calling. "If we haven't been able to reach them on the phone, we keep trying and trying and trying for at least two weeks," Ms. Bowker says. "You can't just call them once."

- Sam Goldsmith of Goldsmith Insurance Agency in Indianapolis: "You've got to be the first guy to call the consumer. If we're working a lead that other people are potentially also going to be calling on, the key is, can I get to that consumer before the next guy? So I'm trying to work in real time. If I'm working in front of my computer, I'm not going to have any background distractions. I'm going to be concentrating on the lead flow and concentrating on dialing."

- Laura Harris of Laura Harris Agency in Corpus Christi, Texas: "In my office, everyone knows the second an Internet lead comes in, they work it instantly." It's the fifth to the seventh call where the customer actually closes the sale; most aren't ready to buy on the first call. Says sending out a hard copy of a quote along with an e-mail copy increased office's closing rate.

On appealing to customers:

- Sam Goldsmith: The key is changing the customer's mind about what agents are and what they do. You have to let the customer know that you're his or her advocate and that it's your job to get that customer the best coverage you can for the best price you can. It's not you who is raising rates or even setting them. Get the customer to think of his or herself as a boxer and of the agent as the manager in the corner, rooting the customer on and helping him or her through to the knockout finish. He says he always asks himself, "Can I get the consumer on the other side of the phone to not think of the agent as a solicitor, as someone trying to take money from them?" There are three things you need to prove if you want to convince the customer that you are, in fact, on his or her side: that you are efficient, that you're not obtrusive or pushy, and that you can offer a fair price.

- Zachary Ebner: Sometimes you'll be competitive, sometimes you won't, depending on how the wind's blowing at the company or companies you sell for. He has a simple piece of advice to deal with that situation, however: "When you're competitive, sell the heck out of (your policies)." Not every customer is going to totally be fixated on price. Some will be, sure, but others are more interested in service and whom they're working with. There are lots of reasons why people look to switch from one agency to another. "Some people love their rate, they just hate their company or hate their agent."

On following up:

- Laura Harris: "It's crucial to be able to stay on top of those leads, and make sure you don't just leave one message and think they're going to be calling you back. The real world does not work that way."

- Cheryl Bowker: You should contact new clients somewhere around six times between the close and their first renewal. That's especially true if you're working with Internet leads. "You have to build a different relationship." You have to prove that you can be personable even if there's some distance between you and the client.

- Zachary Ebner: Follow-ups are a great way to not only make sure everything is in order with the client's policy, paperwork and general well-being, but also to ensure "stickiness" – the quality of a client that determines how easy or difficult it will be to retain him or her well into the future. A great way to ensure that a customer is extra sticky is to sell him or her multiple policies. You can find out if a customer has any interest in other additional policies through following up. Also, you should occasionally call clients – maybe on birthdays or holidays – without an ulterior motive to sell them anything. Just call to send some well wishes. Those displays of goodwill will earn you some goodwill of your own when you call later to talk about policy changes or new offers.

On using a lead management system

- Zachary Ebner: "Without the lead management system, you shouldn't be in this business. If you don't have these automations, you're spinning your wheels."

- Sam Goldsmith: The $50 to $60 per month he pays to keep his database current and keep his subscription to a lead management system going is well worth the cost. Without the automations lead management systems provide, agents now are simply being left behind by those who do use them. "There's not a big overhead."

- Laura Harris: "… It's very difficult to manage all of that if you don't have some type of contact management system. It is so important that we take advantage of not only paying for that lead once, but also following up with that person every six months."

On office management:

- Laura Harris: "You must, must, must separate out your sales people and your service people. If I've got people who are expected to add cars all day long and call on the cancellation audit and do all these other things during the day, and then when an Internet lead pops in, they're expected to drop what they're doing and take care of that, it is extremely, extremely difficult for them to have a good closing ratio. The people who are really good at service typically aren't great at sales, anyway."

- Cheryl Bowker: Makes sure everything happens in her office by standardized processes. In essence, she's automated the workings of her agency's office. "Every agent in my office knows exactly what they're going to do when they arrive in the morning," she said, whether they're contacting new leads, working on retention or writing policies.

- Sam Goldsmith: Works from home. He sees having an office is an unnecessary expense. "I'm working with customers who are shopping online because they don't want to go to someone's office."

Chapter 13:

Making Your Mark

Success is a relative term, and something of a moving target.

Some people define success as simply making a lot of money. Others see it as having a sterling reputation and good standing in your community. Still others think of it in terms of customer satisfaction or sales statistics or awards.

And those are all valid measures of success. But each of those things is simply an aspect of a thriving, healthy business. Ideally, you'll want to be profitable and have continually growing sales numbers while also maintaining a large group of satisfied customers and being well respected among peers and your community at large.

Sounds kind of tough, doesn't it? A lot of plates to spin at one time? It can be, but lots of other agents have achieved such overall success and you can, too. The key is simply using the marketing techniques we have described in the previous chapters – using leads, social networking, referrals – and keeping your finger on the pulse of what's happening in your immediate geographic community, as well as the larger community of insurance agents and your customers.

In other words, get involved. Don't just relegate yourself to your office and maybe a big conference once a year. Go out and make a name for yourself among other insurance agents, your current customers and potential customers. It may take a little time and you may have to spend some of your evenings and weekends working to gain that notoriety, but the dividend will be well worth the investment.

So what are those projects in which you can invest your time to obtain such a return? Here are some ideas.

Join associations. Groucho Marx famously said that he'd never join a club that would have him as a member. It's a funny line, but it also makes the point that membership in an organization assigns someone a sort of immediate status and prestige. Joining local and national trade groups such as the American Insurance Association, the CPCU (Chartered Property Casualty Underwriter) Society, the Group Underwriters Association of America, the Health Insurance Association of America, and the National Association of Insurance and Financial Advisors, gives you instant credibility and puts you in the same category as thousands of other well-respected, prominent and likely profitable agents throughout your state if not the entire country. The dues you pay may seem to not buy you anything, but they do. What they buy you is a direct connection to other agents who have gotten where you want to be.

Go to local networking events. Speaking of connections, there's a lot to be gained from making some at various events in your area where businesspeople of all stripes get together to trade business cards, schmooze and maybe have a meal. It's never a bad thing to let people in your community, especially other business owners, know that you're out there, too. Who knows? You might even convince someone to come in for a meeting or to tell his or her own customers about the service you provide. At the very least, you'll get to know the other people doing business around you, and they'll get to know you, so that when the time comes from those folks to name a local insurance agent, you'll be the name that hits their lips.[47]

Get involved in your area's chamber of commerce. One of the best ways to network with the

---

[47] Found at
http://www.seniormarketadvisor.com/Issues/2008/6/Pag es/The-100-best-marketing-ideas.aspx.

most prominent businesspeople in your city and the surrounding areas is to start attending meetings of your local chamber of commerce – either the larger one or smaller sub-chambers if your area has them. Maybe even consider becoming an officer. It'll show your commitment to your community and cement you as an important member of your local business community. Plus, you'll get to see first-hand what's going on in your community in terms of economic development, which can be a big boon for your agency. For instance, if a new manufacturing plant is coming to your town and with it lots of people moving in from outside the state, that means plenty of potential customers are headed your way, all with similar needs you can be there to help them with.

Find some boards to serve on. A lot of times, agents and other businesspeople will avoid service on boards for fear of being viewed as too political and losing business. And that's a valid concern. There's certainly a risk involved in making statements that could be viewed as controversial, offensive or that could alienate the portion of your customer base that doesn't agree. But service on a board doesn't necessarily mean you have to be so politically outspoken that you alienate customers. It simply means that you get involved in an effort in your community – regarding recycling or building a bike trail, maybe. Something most, if not all, people in the community could get behind.

Sponsor a charity/event/kids' sports team, etc. And in the same vein of events almost everyone can get behind, sponsoring something like a run to cure cancer or a Little League Team or even a local benefit concert can get your agency's name out into the public eye in all the right ways.[48]

Get to know local officials. Much like service on a board, a lot of people blanch at the idea of hanging out with politicians. Often, and understandably so, many folks' first thoughts go directly to bribery, graft and scandal. And it's hard to know which ones are involved in such things and which aren't. But that doesn't mean your interactions with local officials in your town, your county and your state have to go in those directions. There are polite, effective, and best of all, legal, ways to discuss your business, your goals, your industry and local events with the members of your city council, your county commission, state legislature and so on. Simply arrange a visit to his or her office, attend a committee meeting or go to a dinner where such officials might be attending. Introduce yourself. If you've done some of

---

[48] Found at http://www.gaebler.com/Getting-Involved-in-the-Community.htm.

the things listed elsewhere in this chapter, they might even know who you are!

Do some speaking gigs. It can be a little daunting to get in front of a bunch of people in talk. In fact, it's the thing people say they're most afraid of. But you do it every day. You present yourself to customers as simply a matter of course. Getting in front a crowd of people at a luncheon or a Rotary Club meeting to talk about how business is changing or to give the attendees some insurance tips is no different. The audience may be larger, sure, but the art of presentation remains the same. Stay confident, keep your sense of humor and stay loose. That's it. Do those things, and you'll impress everyone in that room.

Organize some lunch meet-ups. Much of what we've listed here so far has to do with you seeking out other people. But you can do just as much by gathering people together. Who? Other agents within your company, if you're a captive agent. If you're an independent agents, other such agents in your area. Or maybe people who work in the industries related to the type of insurance you sell. For instance, if you sell car insurance, maybe you could gather together local car dealers and mechanics to talk about a safety campaign. Or if you're in the health insurance industry, maybe you could get together doctors, nurses and other practitioners to talk about the effects of insurance reform. Whatever group you bring together, you'll prove you have the initiative to get people into a room to talk out solutions to big problems.

Talk up your social media presence. There's a reason we keep bringing up social media and its role in the future of marketing. It really is the way customers are going to find businesses they want to patronize now and for the foreseeable future. So, whenever you see an opportunity, ask people like your page on Facebook. Ask for them to follow you on Twitter. Include addresses for your social media pages on your business card. It may seem like shilling or a bad type of self-promotion, but it's the way business is starting to trend. Get used to it.

If you do all these things, what will you get out of it? Indirectly, you might get new customers, more revenue and a bigger office. You might even get some awards for community involvement or being an agent of the year or something like that. But with enough concentrated, consistent effort you'll reach another level of success, too: You'll become an example that others in your industry want to follow.

We've given you plenty of examples of agents who have used the emerging and new types of marketing that prevail in today's environment to their advantage; maybe one day in the near future, you'll be the agent other people look to as a way to find out how to be a true success in all regards.

Chapter 14:

We Carved Our Own Unique Path and It Has Made All the Difference

By Seth Kravitz

In 2004, my business partner, Lev Barinskiy, got together in a small basement in Columbus, Ohio, and started our company in the hopes of making it easier for insurance agents to get high-quality leads.

That first year was incredibly hard on all of us. We barely made $100,000 in revenue and worked a lot of long hours to do it, but we really believed in what we were doing. My partner Lev's experience with buying bad lead after bad lead for his agency had shown us the poor quality of a lot of the leads out there. We knew we couldn't cut corners and we soon discovered generating high quality leads was a slow process that was going to take time to develop.

By the next year we discovered that we were right to stick with our convictions. In 2005 we had more than doubled our revenue and moved our office into downtown Columbus. By 2007, our revenue had jumped to $750,000, we were hiring new employees and we were big enough to open a marketing office in Chicago.

By 2008, just four years after we started, our revenue had increased by a factor more than 10 from that difficult first year to $12 million. As of 2010, we have signed up more than 8,000 insurance agents in the United States. We went from a few college kids in a basement to one of the largest companies in the lead generation industry.

So how did we get here? We did some things that didn't necessarily conform to the conventional wisdom for how to start a business. We had to throw out some of the old rules of business to make our way in the new landscape the Web has facilitated. In some cases, we had to do the exact opposite of the conventional business wisdom.

Here's a rundown of some things we have been doing to grow, sustain that growth, and create a solid company:

Don't waste time on unnecessary meetings. Meetings sometimes do more harm than they do good. They're not terribly productive, since a series of reply-all e-mails could get across the same information to everyone who needs it. An hour-long meeting uses up an hour of everyone's productivity – and not every bit of information in the meeting is going to involve every person there. They easily drift off-topic to someone talking about his or her vacation. They often don't work. And if you feel it's imperative to have a meeting, don't waste a full hour. If it only takes a few minutes to get the information needed across, only take those few minutes and only include the people that really need to be there.

Streamline. You should keep your business growing, but that doesn't mean your office should balloon up out of proportion. Consider closely when you make hires just how necessary the position is. Are you working with as little as you need to get the job done well? Any more than that is just bloat, and you should cut it out.

Do more with less. Instead of throwing time and money into an ever-growing sinkhole of a problem, try coming up with smaller, more elegant solutions. Sometimes, that solution might be scrapping the project entirely. And that's OK. You should make those tough calls and avoid wasting time on things that won't be successes. Focus on those things you can do well and don't worry yourself with trying to sell customers something you're not an expert on or that isn't up to your standards.

Don't cut out the good stuff. As your agency grows, it's inevitable that your business plan will change. And that's a good thing. It's worthwhile to try new things and blaze new trails. But it's imperative that you remember to not get rid of what works. Change for the sake of change itself is not a good thing, especially if it results in the loss of the things that made your business plan work in the first place.

Find the fastest solution. Complex problems require complex solutions, right? Not necessarily. While your competitors are trying to piece through a puzzle, you should be figuring out ways to deal with your problems the quickest way possible. Think outside the box, but also think in terms of ease, speed and being able to power through the problem so you can focus on more important things. Is there a piece of software, a service, or a product you can buy that will save you hours of time per week? Than it is most likely worth the cost. Your time is the most valuable asset you have in a business.

Don't copy your competitors. I realize this entire book is about techniques and tips from successful agents, but don't simply copy their ideas line for line. It seems almost instinctual to most businesspeople: Copy what your successful competitors do so that you can replicate their success. But that's faulty thinking. Just because someone else turned an idea into big success doesn't mean you'll get the same result from it. Different companies gain success in different ways. And why is that? It's because different businesses have different personalities. They appeal to different groups of people. That means what one agent is doing to gain new business might be a terrible fit for your agency and you need to figure out a way to adapt the concept to fit your agency.

Be real. A big complaint among a lot of businesspeople, especially those who have to work with customers, is that they feel they have to put on some sort of very serious, very professional facade to be able to talk to customers. They hate not being able to be themselves, have a sense of humor and talk frankly. But why not? A little looseness and humor isn't unprofessional, as long as you don't say anything inappropriate. You know what the line is; just don't cross it. Loosen up. As long as you sense they are comfortable with it, talk to the customer like a friend of yours. It'll make everyone more comfortable.

Take a strong stand. We've found the best way to get people to not just like what you're doing, but love it, is to have strong opinions about why you're in the industry you're in, what it does and what your products ought to be. Of course, strong opinions will turn some people off, but you're not trying to appeal to everyone. You are trying to find clients that will renew and stay with you for a long time. And we're not talking about things like politics and world events here, we're specifically talking about your opinions about your business, how it's run and what it provides.

Your products are not the best fit for every single person that you reach and the more upfront and honest you are about whom your insurance policies are designed for, the better clients you will have. You can't please everyone.

Apologize like a human being. <u>Everyone makes mistakes</u>. So why, when you send out a letter of apology or email or make an apologetic phone call, do you end up sounding like a robot? "I'm sorry for any inconvenience this may have caused" not only downplays any problem your customer may have had, it also just sounds insincere. Own up to the failure completely (no blaming anyone but yourself) and in plain, simple words, say you're sorry for the mistake.

Use a personal touch. As we've discussed, the traditional walls between what's business and what's personal are coming down, or at the very least becoming thinner and being pushed back. Now, we're not saying that you should pry into your customers' private lives or show up to their houses uninvited, but it will show them you care if you take an interest in their lives. Let them give you all the information you're comfortable giving, and tell them some things about yourself, too. Distance is overrated.

Own the news about your agency, even if it's bad. Don't try to cover up your mistakes. Eventually, the news will get out; word of mouth is incredibly powerful these days (think email and Facebook). Who would you prefer telling the story? Someone you trust, such as yourself, or a stranger? If there's a problem, own up to it. And tell your customers how it happened from your perspective. People will appreciate the candor and you can make sure the truth gets out into the public.[49]

Tell your compelling story. Business successes like Gary Vaynerchuk, a wine expert who turned a video blog and social networking into a booming wine sales business, say personal branding is one of the biggest keys to really making a dent in the new marketing world. And one of the biggest parts of your personal brand is your story. Everyone has one. We gave you a brief version of ours at the start of this chapter. You may think yours is too boring for people to be interested in it, but a lot of the response will depend on how you tell it. Present your story with the right amount of enthusiasm and people will flock to hear it. [50]

Everyone wants to hear about successes. Especially all of us here at InsuranceAgents.com. If you have a fun story to tell or have a great success you would like to share, let us know. We would love to

---

[49] Fried, Jason and Hansson, David Heinemeier. *Rework.* 2010.
[50] Vaynerchuk, Gary. *Crush It!: Why Now is the Time to Cash in on Your Passion.* 2009.

share your experiences on our website and with our thousands of agents.

I hope you have enjoyed reading this book as much as we enjoyed writing it. This was a work of passion and I really hope you took away at least one tip you can use to grow your agency. As I said at the beginning of the book, if you ever have any questions, concerns, or suggestions, you can email us at support@insuranceagents.com.

GLOSSARY

blog An online publication, by one author or multiple authors, that provides news, opinion, or may act as a public journal. Entries often include links to other websites.

customer relationship management The business practice of keeping up with client needs and expectations in a systematic way. Methods of such management include follow ups, sending newsletters, e-mail updates or seeking suggestions. A lead management system from a source such as AgencyIQ, ALISS, EZLynx, Vertafore, Typhoon, Mojo, InsideSales.com, Prospector+, Leads360 or Imprezzio will help with the process.

desktop publishing Publication design and production using personal computers.

Facebook A social media website which allows users to interact with friends, post messages, post photos, play games and view organizations' information pages. Those pages allow users to communicate with those organizations, including businesses.

follow To put another Twitter user's tweets into your timeline. Example: *"I just followed InsuranceAgents.com on Twitter and now I can see their tweets on my main Twitter page."*

follower Someone who has your tweets in his/her Twitter timeline.

friend Term for another user on Facebook with whom one shares information, status updates and links, and whose own updates appear in one's news feed. Though the term is "friend," a Facebook friend could be a family member, co-worker, acquaintance, classmate, business associate or even a stranger.

group A Facebook and LinkedIn feature that allows users to join other like-minded users on various topics. Once users join a group, they may share information among each other or invite others to join the group. For instance, an insurance agent in Ohio could start the group "Ohio Insurance Agents" and invite other users who fall into that category.

guerrilla marketing Small-scale promotional efforts that focus on imaginative concepts and interactivity.

One example of a guerrilla marketing idea is "astroturfing," a method of getting groups of people to publicly rally in favor of a product or service.

hashtag A word or phrase with no spaces and starting with "#." Used to make tweets about the same topic easily searchable. Example: *"I just read InsuranceAgents.com's new book! #insuranceinfo"*

integrated marketing The strategy of using various marketing methods such as mass media, direct marketing and guerilla marketing, together to bolster one another and produce market data.

lead Information that identifies a potential customer. Such information may come in a number of different ways, including e-mails, phone calls, text messages, direct mail, or printouts.

lead management The use of a software program or online application to organize leads and automatically make follow ups.

like How Facebook users become a fan of a page or show their approval for a post. Accomplished by clicking the "like" button. A user becomes a fan of your agency's page by liking it.

LinkedIn A social media website for business professionals. Members use the site to look for jobs, list job openings, recommend businesses, join groups and post photos.

mass media A means of communicating messages to a the general public. Often refers to television, radio, newspapers and magazines.

news feed A stream of Facebook friends' status updates as well as updates from various Facebook pages.

page A Facebook hub businesses and others can create as a place where fans of that organization can post comments or respond to messages.

private message A Twitter feature that allows users to send tweets that are only available to one other user rather than all of his/her other followers.

profile A Facebook or LinkedIn user's personal space on the social media site where he/she can post updates and see others' responses to those updates.

recommend How LinkedIn users state their approval of another professional who uses the site.

retweet A way Twitter users can show their approval for or respond to another user's tweet by repeating it.

social media Websites or applications that allow users to create content, exchange it and provide feedback for other users' content. Facebook itself is a social media website.

social networking The practice of using social media to connect with other users. Using Facebook is social networking.

spam Unsolicited messages, usually advertisements or commercial offers, sent in bulk. Often refers to e-mails, but can apply to other electronic and non-electronic messages as well.

timeline The collection of all the tweets of everyone a Twitter user follows.

tweet A message posted to Twitter.

Twitter A social networking website that allows users to post short messages of 140 characters or less.

viral marketing A technique by which videos, clips, images and other content gets passed around among users online so that it is seen by huge audiences.

YouTube The world's most popular video site; users can post videos, view videos and leave comments.

7057240R0

Made in the USA
Lexington, KY
15 October 2010